1001
GREATEST
THINGS
EVER SAID
ABOUT
MASSACHUSETTS

Edited and with an Introduction by
Patricia Harris and David Lyon

THE LYONS PRESS
Guilford, Connecticut
An imprint of The Globe Pequot Press

For the patient and knowledgeable staff of the Cambridge Public
Library and the Minuteman Library Network

The Lyons Press is an imprint of Morris Book Publishing, LLC

10 9 8 7 6 5 4 3 2 1

Printed in the United States of America

Designed by Carol Sawyer/Rose Design

ISBN 978-1-59921-096-4

Library of Congress Cataloging-in-Publication Data is available on file.

To buy books in quantity for corporate use
or incentives, call **(800) 962–0973**
or e-mail **premiums@GlobePequot.com.**

Contents

It is a State of tradition, but part of its tradition is its history of revolt.

—WPA Guide to Massachusetts

INTRODUCTION

*T*oo bad that Massachusetts author Ralph Waldo Emerson was constitutionally incapable of irony. For the man who wrote, "I hate quotations. Tell me what you know," also penned innumerable epigrammatic quips on the state of Massachusetts, the state of Concord spiritual life, or, for that matter, the state of the universe. He had an opinion on everything and rarely hid his light under a bushel.

Besides, he probably didn't mean to diss quotations—and if he did, he could easily have changed his mind. "A foolish consistency is the hobgoblin of little minds," he once wrote. The Sage of Concord and his many three-named friends (Henry David Thoreau, Louisa May Alcott, Oliver Wendell Holmes, Henry Wadsworth Longfellow) were rarely short of insights, as the pages to follow amply illustrate.

Alas, Massachusetts can't claim the great English lexicographer Samuel Johnson, but one of his observations bears repeating: "Every quotation contributes something to the stability and enlargement of the language." Emerson and company didn't have the last word, even in Massachusetts, where the American vernacular is enlarged and stabilized almost daily by everyone from politicians indulging in their characteristic invective to traffic reporters inventing new words and phrases to describe the singular horrors of Massachusetts roadways. (Massachusetts driving is sometimes described as "a contact sport." The subject deserves, and receives, its own chapter.)

The individual quotations in this book can be heart-wrenching, profound, amusing, clever, brave, reverent or simply true. Each stands alone as a thought. But in the aggregate, they begin to create a mosaic of Massachusetts the state, the people, and the state of mind.

Bay Staters are Plymouth Rock-steady in embracing their creation myth as pioneers seeking religious freedom in the wilderness. As theologian Wendell Phillips observed of those forefathers and foremothers, "What the Puritans gave the world was not thought, but action." Most Massachusetts folk remain convinced, more than a century after James Russell Lowell observed it, that "Puritanism, believing itself quick with the seed of religious liberty, laid, without knowing it, the egg of democracy."

Revolution must have been in the genes. Massachusetts "is a state of tradition, but part of its tradition is its history of revolt," as the authors of the WPA guide to the state noted in 1937. Bay Staters were the rabble-rousers of the American Revolution, saying so many pithy things about giving the king the boot that we found it was impossible to contain them save in an independent chapter.

Massachusetts has been on the barricades ever since, priding itself on being (these days) the bluest of the blue states, where the term

"Massachusetts liberal" seems to be redundant. The Bay State's social and political locus on the left bank of American thought is hardly new. In the 1860s, recalled Washington Gladden, "North Adams was, indeed, a good example of a New England democracy. All its traditions were of an uncompromising radicalism." When Richard Nixon won re-election by a landslide, Massachusetts cast the dissenting vote. Bay Staters still proclaim, "Don't blame me. I'm from Massachusetts."

That faint air of superiority perhaps originates in the state capital, Boston, variously described as "City on a Hill," "Athens of America," and "city of smarties." Education has long dominated Massachusetts life, beginning with the nation's first college, Harvard. "To this day the Proper Bostonian never ceases to wonder at the large number of young men who, apparently happily, attend colleges other than Harvard," observed Cleveland Amory in 1947. Higher education is central to the Massachusetts identity. Businessman Jack Connors reported in 2004 that "Someone once asked me how you could replicate what we have. I told them, 'Build two world-class universities and wait 100 years.'"

Passionate minds have passionate appetites. Bay Staters have distinct ideas about the importance of baked beans and how a proper chowder must be prepared. As New England travel enthusiast and author Eleanor Early sniffed, "Tomatoes and clams have no more affinity than ice cream and horseradish. It is a sacrilege to wed bivalves with bay leaves, and only a degraded cook would do such a thing." The mingling of tomato and clams is prima facie evidence that the cook is a Manhattan sympathizer.

Likewise, in sporting matters, a ferocious rivalry endures between Boston and New York, going back at least to the 86-year drought of baseball world championships attributed to the "Curse of the Bambino." Win or lose, Red Sox Nation remains faithful, and the players know it. "I played before the greatest fans in baseball, the Boston fans," Ted Williams finally admitted in his 1969 autobiography, *My Turn at Bat*. Nor do Bay Staters limit their devotion to the baseball diamond. "The Celtics aren't a team. They're a way of life," Red Auerbach always contended. Massachusetts fans bring equal passion to individual sports as to team efforts. Four-time winner of the Boston Marathon Bill Rodgers calls the race fans "the best crowds of any marathon in the world."

Over its long-running history, Massachusetts has been populated by more than its share of colorful and controversial characters who have uttered sagacious thoughts (excerpted here in the "Memorable Lines" chapter) while serving as the subject for observation by others (which is a chapter unto itself). John F. Kennedy, for example, was one of the great wordsmiths of his era, but Lyndon Johnson also nailed him when he called the then-senator "the enviably attractive nephew who sings an Irish ballad for the company and then winsomely disappears before the table-clearing and dishwashing begin."

Bay Staters have rarely been at a loss for words, hymning paeans of praise to the streets and houses of their cities and towns, the grand achievements of their stages, musicians, writers, and painters, and the sublime pleasures of a landscape varied enough to satisfy the desires of a country, let alone a state. Each subject is duly noted in the following pages in the hopes that this compendium can aspire to W.E.B. Du Bois's definition of a classic: "a book that doesn't have to be written again."

Patricia Harris and David Lyon
Cambridge, Massachusetts
December 2006

DON'T BLAME ME

Massachusetts political and social leanings

Don't Blame me. I'm from Massachusetts.

—*Post-Watergate bumper sticker*

Democrats make up the state's entire delegation of congressmen and senators; among voters, Democrats outnumber Republicans three to one; Republicans hold just 29 of 200 seats in the state's House and Senate combined; and a Republican has not served as mayor of Boston since 1937. All of which explains why Massachusetts is largely viewed by the rest of America as a sort of Marxist redoubt with great seafood.

—*Noel C. Paul*

Being a conservative Republican in Massachusetts is a bit like being a cattle rancher at a vegetarian convention.

—*Mitt Romney*

Many symbols have been devised to explain the Bay Stater. He has been pictured as a kind of dormant volcano, the red-hot lava from one eruption hardening into a crater which impedes the next; as a river, with two main currents of transcendental metaphysics and catchpenny opportunism running side by side; as an asocial discord consisting mainly of overtones and undertones; as a petrified backbone, "that unblossoming stalk."

—*WPA guide to Massachusetts*

The Inhabitants [of Massachusetts] seem very Religious, showing many outward and visible signs of an inward and Spiritual Grace: But tho' they wear in their Faces the Innocence of Doves, you will find them in their Dealings as Subtile as Serpents. Interest is their Faith, Money their God, and Large Possessions the only Heaven they covet.

—*Edward Ward*

I loved the juicy ethnic mix of Massachusetts politics. Boston's Irish Mafia constantly reminded me of the Irish in Australian political life—the rhetoric and invective flowed in a different accent but the passion and the genius for political maneuvering were the same.

—*Jill Ker Conway*

Politics, as a practice, whatever its professions, had always been the systematic organization of hatreds, and Massachusetts politics had been as harsh as the climate.

—*Henry Adams*

[O]nly people who have witnessed Town Meeting Day in an isolated Berkshire Hill town can appreciate its significance. . . . Major political parties don't come in for much attention . . . for it's all a matter of "one side" and the "other side." Personal grievances and vague prejudices are usually the platforms adopted by the "sides."

—WPA Guide to The Berkshire Hills

Presidential candidates may well be Massachusetts' most popular export. . . . To be sure, our intellectually geared culture is known for hatching innovations in health care and high tech, but it also does so in politics and public policy, making us a breeding ground for smart ideas and new leadership. The result: Massachusetts matters.

—*Tom Keane*

But to view the national stage from Massachusetts is to know the bitter truth that our state plays an important role in America's political theater. Every two years, bluest blue Massachusetts sends in the clowns. We show America what could be and America generally sees it and acts accordingly: runs in the other direction.

—Jules Crittenden

To hear [George W. Bush] tell it, Massachusetts is not a state now on its fourth Republican governor in a row or one with one of the lowest tax burdens in the country . . . but some sort of Sodom on the Bay, with 90 percent tax rates, mandatory Wicca ceremonies in public schools, and an anarcho-syndicalist majority in the state legislature. How could "real" Americans be expected to accept a candidate from such a place?

—Paul Waldman

In 20 years as a senator from Massachusetts, [John Kerry] has built a record of—of a senator from Massachusetts.

—George W. Bush

The enduring qualities of Massachusetts—the common threads woven by the Pilgrim and the Puritan, the fisherman and the farmer, the Yankee and the immigrant—will not be and could not be forgotten in the Nation's Executive Mansion. They are an indelible part of my life, my convictions, my view of the past, my hopes for the future.

—John F. Kennedy

There's nothing that scares people more than when you say "San Francisco liberal" or "Massachusetts liberal."

—Carl Forti

Next time Massachusetts speaks, listen!

—Post-Watergate bumper sticker

We're liberals, we don't have guns, but don't make me go in the back room and grab my yoga mat, because trust me, you don't want me in the downward dog position.

—Massachusetts comedian Jimmy Tingle

Massachusetts is way out on a limb. . . . It already has a kooky reputation in the rest of the country. There is no doubt about that.

—Former Republican Congressman Peter I. Blute

And the Massachusetts liberals will be going to the World Series!
                                    —*Tom Toles editorial cartoon*

Proud to be a
latte sipping
Volvo driving
sushi eating
liberal from
Blue America

                                    —*Massachusetts bumper sticker*

North Adams was, indeed, a good example of a New England
democracy. All its traditions were of an uncompromising radicalism.
                                    —*Washington Gladden*

If ever there was a symbol for the essence of Massachusetts . . . who could trump this eight-term senator [Edward M. Kennedy] who stands his ground as a lightning rod for criticism from the wicked heartless conservative establishment?

—Jennifer Graham

You're from Massachusetts if you think the Kennedys are misunderstood.

—Bay State humor

People are always amazed to learn that conservatives live here in Massachusetts. They wonder what that can be like. It can be galling to think that, in presidential elections, your vote doesn't count.

—Jules Crittenden

I think that our party, in political terms, is largely irrelevant.
— *former Massachusetts Republican Governor William Weld*

The Spirit of America

                    — *motto on the state's license plate*

The ability of Massachusetts politicians to generate national ridicule for this state is renowned. Michael Dukakis and the tank will always be No. 1, though Paul Tsongas in a Speedo should never be that far behind. Bill Weld's full-clothed plunge into the Charles proves bipartisanship lives when it comes to wacky headlines. But for sheer imagery nothing matches [Jarrett] Barrios' call to limit school servings of Marshmallow Fluff in schools. . . .

                    — *Baystateliberal blog*

This tailgate is a Time—which is what Massachusetts politicians throw whenever they must once again run for office. . . . A Time is usually a fund-raising dinner, but it can be a fund-raising lunch, a fund-raising trip to the ballpark, or yes, a fund-raising wake, where, very likely, Jimbo Jr. will be shaking hands over the departed Jimbo Sr. preparatory to a run for the Governor's Council.

—*Charles P. Pierce*

I wonder who passed the Massachusetts law mandating that incumbents get their names listed first on the ballot? Why . . . it was the incumbents. Surprise, surprise.

—*Malia Zimmerman*

Politics and holiness are not always synonymous. There are times . . . when, if you wish to win an election, you must first do unto others as they wish to do unto you, but you must do it first.

> —*Massachusetts politician James Michael Curley*

Skillful of hand, sharp at a bargain, stubborn of mind, the Bay Stater possesses a character which with its mixture of shrewdness and idealism is often labeled hypocrisy.

> —WPA Guide to Massachusetts

All politics is local.

> —*Thomas P. "Tip" O'Neill*

South Boston was, and arguably still is, the most politically active community in Massachusetts. It abounds both in widely known politicians and aspirants lusting to replace them in office. . . . Politics was a cottage industry, a spectator sport and, I suppose, the nearest thing we had to a real-life drama, sitcom or game show.

— *William M. Bulger*

Certain Irish-American families—the Kennedys predominant among them—have Massachusetts politics sewn up, to the benefit of one ethnic group, more than prevails anywhere else in the immensely complicated ethnic and clan politics of the U.S.

— *Conor Cruise O'Brien*

The major candidates for governor here have signature attributes of generations of Massachusetts politicians. They have Irish surnames and Harvard degrees, and both rose to financial prosperity from humbler origins.

—*Pam Belluck*

It says something encouraging about American democracy that even in this tribal state, where politics can be hard to distinguish from blood feuds and the old pols' network jealously takes care of its own, a black kid from the slums—the Chicago slums, at that—can grow up to be governor.

—*Jeff Jacoby*

We are a great state. We have a tradition of innovation and economic leadership, a concentration of brainpower and venture capital, beautiful land- and seascapes, and extraordinary people. But yesterday's greatness will not guarantee tomorrow's.

—Governor Deval Patrick

If I were a Democrat, I suspect I'd feel a heck of a lot more comfortable in Boston than, say, America.

—Congressman Richard "Dick" Armey

The people of Boston are rich in their inheritances that are good to cultivate and or transmit. What shall be winnowed out of them all for posterity, none may say. There is yet no reason to fear a discontinuance of that state of mind which is informed peculiarly with the fruitful qualities of responsibility and rebellion.

—Mark De Wolfe Howe

He comes from the Brahmin caste of New England. This is the harmless, inoffensive, untitled aristocracy . . . with their houses by Bulfinch, their monopoly of Beacon Street, their ancestral portraits and Chinese porcelains, humanitarianism, Unitarian faith in the march of the mind, Yankee shrewdness, and New England exclusiveness.

—Oliver Wendell Holmes

We are all a little wild here with numerous projects of social reform.

—Ralph Waldo Emerson

Clubs of female faddists, old gentlemen with disordered livers, or pessimists croaking over imaginary good old days and ignoring the sunlit present.

—James Michael Curley, on Boston Brahmins

Boston runs to brains as well as to beans and brown bread. But she is cursed with an army of cranks whom nothing short of a straitjacket or a swamp elm club will ever control.

—*William Cowper Brown*

Yet Boston has never lost her universal supremacy for being independent in character, original in enterprise, unwilling to follow whenever she is reasonably equipped to lead.

—*David McCord*

Full of crooked little streets; but I tell you, Boston has opened and kept open more turnpikes that lead straight to free thought and free speech and free deeds than any other city of live men or dead men.

—*Oliver Wendell Holmes, Jr.*

PROUDLY WEAR YOUR LOYALTY TO PROGRESSIVE
VALUES AND THE BAY STATE RIGHT ABOVE YOUR
BLEEDING HEART!

—trueblueliberal.org,
a website devoted to "reclaiming America, one state at a time"

The Massachusetts Constitution coined the phrase "we the people"
. . . and the people of Massachusetts lived up to it. So let's toast the
people of Massachusetts—North, East, South and West—for their
singular role in devising the oldest constitution in the western world!

—Mark D. Mason

The question before us is whether, consistent with the Massachusetts Constitution, the Commonwealth may deny the protections, benefits, and obligations conferred by civil marriage to two individuals of the same sex who wish to marry. We conclude that it may not. The Massachusetts Constitution affirms the dignity and equality of all individuals. It forbids the creation of second-class citizens.

—Massachusetts chief justice Margaret H. Marshall

Here in Massachusetts, activist judges struck a blow to the foundation of civilization, the family. They ruled that our constitution requires same sex marriage.

—Governor Mitt Romney

I am a citizen of Massachusetts where gay people have been getting married for two years without the sky falling.

—Ellen Goodman

Nobody in the [Massachusetts] Legislature who supported gay marriage lost their jobs, and the Boston Red Sox won the World Series. And the crops came up, and the locusts stayed away.

—*Matt Foreman*

Obviously, Salem's enthusiastic embrace of the supernatural makes it a tempting target for religious zealots. So does the fact that Salem has one of the largest per capita populations (however diverse) of practicing neo-pagans anywhere in the world. . . . And, not surprising, many of the practitioners—independent, liberal, and otherwise iconoclastic women—happen to be pro-choice. If the right has a well-established flair for demonizing the left, in Salem the demonization is literal.

—*David J. Skal*

When the culture is sick, every element in it becomes infected.
While it is no excuse for this [clerical sex] scandal, it is no surprise
that Boston, a seat of academic, political, and cultural liberalism in
America, lies at the center of the storm.

—Senator Rick Santorum

As the home of Henry David Thoreau and Frederick Law Olmsted,
Massachusetts has long enjoyed a reputation as one of the greenest
states.

—Boston Globe *editorial*

Massachusetts Tree Hugger

—bumper sticker

[T]he Bay State became a "nanny state" well before the term was born. In the 1630s, the General Court prescribed dress codes for citizens and imposed wage and price controls. . . . In 1894, well before the advent of automobiles, Massachusetts implemented an array of restrictions on bicycle riding. . . . And long before Prohibition (or the abolition of "happy hour" in the 1980s), the state had banned the sale of liquor to anyone receiving public assistance.

—*Robert David Sullivan*

The average parent may, for example, plant an artist or fertilize a ballet dancer and end up with a certified public accountant. We cannot train children along chicken wire to make them grow in the right direction. Tying them to stakes is frowned upon, even in Massachusetts.

—*Ellen Goodman*

Probably there is not a community on the face of the earth that is so over-legislated . . . nor a community anywhere which tolerates such petty, inconsequential, and unnecessary legislation.

—Massachusetts attorney general Albert Pillsbury

[T]he Commonwealth of Massachusetts instituted the suit that ultimately found its way here, praying that the book [*The Memoirs of Fanny Hill*] be declared obscene so that the citizens of Massachusetts might be spared the necessity of determining for themselves whether or not to read it.

—Justice William O. Douglas

reliable redoubt of liberal caricatures

—Kate Zernike, on Massachusetts

WARNING
Massachusetts State House
Fiscally Responsible Should Turn Back

—GOPnews.blog.com

Taxachusetts

—George H.W. Bush

Massachusetts: Lower Taxes than Sweden

—bumper sticker

You're from Massachusetts if you understand why they call it Taxachusetts.

—Bay State humor

Actually, because I was born and raised in Rhode Island, I've known for many years that Massachusetts politicians were, let's say, a few votes short of a caucus. But now the state is looking at mandating the electronic file formats that its office productivity workers can use!

—Dave Kearns

We, here in Massachusetts, are stubbornly loyal. Hell, we're Red Sox and Patriots fans and that loyalty paid off.

—Robert Parks

Here in Massachusetts, we're doing better than just about anywhere else in the country in living our private lives as we wish.

—Harvey Silverglate

If you could only see
I know you would agree
There ain't nowhere else to be
But Massachusetts

—State Folk Song by Arlo Guthrie

THE HUB

Boston

Boston is what I would like the whole United States to be.

—*Charles Dickens*

For we must consider that we shall be as a City on a Hill. The eyes of all people are upon us.

—*Governor John Winthrop*

Boston's ruling class as it approached the late nineteenth century did not doubt then (any more than does its more diverse elite today), that it was leading Puritan Governor John Winthrop's visionary city on a hill, America's first and brightest beacon, always testing, measuring, valuing, illuminating. There was no more judgmental place anywhere.

—*Douglass Shand-Tucci*

Tonight I appear for the first time before a Boston audience—
4,000 critics.

—*Mark Twain*

If Columbus had landed on the West Coast, Boston would never
have been heard of.

—*Mark De Wolfe Howe, quoting a "westerner" on a train*

I do not speak with any fondness but the language of the coolest
history, when I say that Boston commands attention as the town
which was appointed in the destiny of nations to lead the civilization
of North America.

—*Ralph Waldo Emerson*

There has never been anything quite like Boston as a creation of the American imagination, or perhaps one should say as a creation of the American scene. Some of the legend was once real, surely.

—*Elizabeth Hardwick*

I feel very strongly that I was sent to Boston, directed there, because it was in Boston that I met Martin Luther King, Jr.

—*Coretta Scott King*

Boston was one of the most American of cities. It was a community that tried to embody and institutionalize an idea.

—*Martin Green*

I guess God made Boston on a wet Sunday.

—Raymond Chandler

Boston is the only city in America you could satirize.

—John P. Marquand

Boston is the perfect city for the Democrats, 'cause the Democrats are like the Red Sox. They're optimistic in the spring, concerned in the summer, and ready to choke in the fall.

—Jay Leno

America's foremost city of words, Boston has, in turn, articulated the nation's sense of the past, mapped its symbolic landscape, and shaped its moral quest.

—Shaun O'Connell

[The TV show] *Cheers* [brought Boston] more fame than Paul Revere's ride, as much hometown pride as the Boston Red Sox and more pseudo-intellectualism, if you can believe that, than a Harvard Square café.

—Governor William Weld

Strong surroundings allow strong characters, and Boston has its share of both.

—Jane Holtz Kay

Every real Boston family has a sea-captain in its background.
—*Thomas Appleton*

The society of Boston was and is quite uncivilized but refined beyond
the point of civilization.
—*T. S. Eliot*

And this is good old Boston,
The home of the bean and the cod,
Where the Lowells talk only to the Cabots,
And the Cabots talk only to God.
—*John Collins Bossidy*

Boston is the headquarters of Cant. Notwithstanding its superior intelligence, its large provision of benevolent institutions, and its liberal hospitality, there is an extraordinary and most pernicious union, in more than a few scattered instances, of profligacy and the worst kind of infidelity, with a strict religious profession, and an outward demeanour of remarkable propriety.

—*Harriet Martineau*

A solid man of Boston.
A comfortable man with dividends,
And the first salmon and the first green peas.

—*Henry Wadsworth Longfellow*

In Boston the night comes down with an incredibly heavy, small-town finality. The cows come home; the chickens go to roost; the meadow is dark. Nearly every Bostonian is in his house or in some-one else's house, dining at the home board, enjoying domestic and social privacy.

—*Elizabeth Hardwick*

Clothes, budgetary bane of women of lesser mettle, have never proved so to the Boston woman. A familiar legend is the story of the lady who, asked by an amazed visitor to Boston where Boston women get their hats, replied: "Our hats? Why we have our hats."

—*Cleveland Amory*

The elegant women are between Arlington and Berkeley [streets], and I don't know where they go after then.

—*Smoki Bacon*

[A Boston gentleman] gets up leisurely, breakfasts comfortably, reads the paper regularly, dresses fashionably, eats a tart gravely, talks insipidly, dines considerably, drinks superfluently, kills time indifferently, sups elegantly, goes to bed stupidly and lives uselessly.

—*Boston Transcript,* 1832

[Boston is] a city where any man is deemed best-dressed who resists buying suits with two pairs of pants.

—*George Frazier*

For a woman to dress too smartly in Boston is to open herself to the charge that she is a social climber.

—*Cleveland Amory*

The State-House is the hub of the solar system.

—Oliver Wendell Holmes

Nobody quite remembers how this Hub of Universe business got started. Boston has never been at the geographical center of anything, and its moment as a historical nexus had peaked before the Civil War. And yet, it is still considered—and certainly considers itself—a cosmopolitan city.

—John Powers

My mother felt a horrified giddiness about the adventure of our address. . . . We were less than fifty yards from Louisburg Square, the cynosure of old historic Boston's plain-spoken, cold-roast elite—the Hub of the Hub of the Universe. Fifty yards!

—Robert Lowell

[Beacon Hill] has the entire city at its fingertips.

—*Robin Cook*

There is a city in our world upon which the light of the sun of righteousness has risen. There is a sun which beams in its full meridian splendor upon it. Its influences are quickening and invigorating the souls that dwell within it. It is the same from which every pure stream of thought and purpose and performance emanates. It is the city that is set on high. It cannot be hid. It is Boston!

—*Bronson Alcott*

[Beacon Hill's North slope] is where *Satan's seat* is. . . . Here, week after week, whole nights are spent in drinking and carousing; and as the morning light begins to appear, when others arise from their beds, these close their doors. . . . Here in one compact section of the town, it is confidently affirmed and fully believed, there are *three hundred females* wholly devoid of shame and modesty. . . .

—*Reverend James Davis, 1817*

Boston is absolutely nothing to me—I don't even dislike it. I like it, on the contrary: I only dislike to live there.

—*Henry James*

I have just returned from Boston. It is the only sane thing to do if you find yourself up there.

—*Fred Allen*

Crossing a bare common, in snow puddles at twilight, under a clouded sky, without having in my thoughts any occurrence of special good fortune, I have enjoyed a perfect exhilaration.

—Ralph Waldo Emerson

The city is a beautiful one and cannot fail, I should imagine, to impress all strangers very favorably.

—Charles Dickens

Certainly no other American city can boast a slice of the wilderness so tinctured with history as the fabulous area bounded by Beacon, Park, Tremont, Boylston, and Charles streets.

—David McCord

I am sure you would like England very much, it is a paradise, but so I think is Boston Common.

—*John Singleton Copley*

Even more important than the State House as a central feature of old Boston is the Common—resort of the populace from the days of the Puritans, playground of boys and girls of nearly three centuries, favorite pasture of the gentle Boston cow for more than half that time. The fifty acres that slope gently down Beacon Street from the State House to Boylston and Tremont Streets have been jealously guarded from all intrusion.

—*John T. Faris*

Boston was in a manner of its own stoutly and vividly urban, not only a town, but a town of history.

—*Henry James*

Boston remains a place where older is frequently seen as better. There are old houses, old churches, old shops, old cemeteries, old hotels, old roadways, an old harbor, old playgrounds and parks. Boston is notoriously a place were "antiques" are much admired (and sought after).

—*John Demos*

Boston, you must remember, is not a city to be trifled with. If it chooses to sleep, it can be very nasty when forcefully awakened. Its temper is like its weather, which is conducive to sleep; and with all these naps, Boston is unusually strongly armed during its waking hours. Its resistance to change and artistic progress is phenomenal.

—*Leonard Bernstein*

Whoever has been down to the end of Long Wharf and walked through Quincy Market has seen Boston.

—*Henry David Thoreau*

The fact that Boston's past touches us daily is the most modern thing about the city.

—*Benjamin Thompson*

Clear out 800,000 people and preserve it as a museum piece.

—*Frank Lloyd Wright*

Despite its venerable status, Boston has never allowed itself to be converted into a historical shrine or an antiquarian museum preserved in all its colonial splendor.

—*Thomas H. O'Connor*

Boston's history is a huge asset. . . . It is the urban equivalent of going to a national park. . . . History is one of the most magical things about it.

—*Janet Marie Smith*

It was my habit to go very slowly up the low, broad steps to the palace entrance, pleasing my eyes with the majestic lines of the building, and lingering to read again the carved inscriptions: Public Library—Built by the People—Free to All.

—*Mary Antin*

The main entrance to the Boston Public Library used to face Copley
Square across Dartmouth Street. . . . It felt like a library and looked
like a library, and even when I was going in there to look up Duke
Snider's lifetime batting average, I used to feel like a scholar.

                                                    —*Robert B. Parker*

I see a great many barrels and fig-drums—piles of wood for umbrella-
sticks, —blocks of granite and ice, —great heaps of goods, and the
means of packing and conveying them, —much wrapping-paper
and twine, —many crates and hogsheads and trucks, —and that
is Boston. The more barrels, the more Boston. The museums and
scientific societies and libraries are accidental.

                                                    —*Henry David Thoreau*

The outstretched fingers of the great Boston wharves still carry the
old romance in their length and look.

—*David McCord*

In Boston they ask How much does he know? In New York, How
much is he worth? In Philadelphia, who were his parents?

—*Mark Twain*

All I claim for Boston is that it is the thinking center of the continent,
and therefore of the planet.

—*Oliver Wendell Holmes*

Boston, unlike Chicago, is not a city of broad shoulders. To state the obvious, its claim to fame has been its intellectual capital, which has not always matched its towering intellectual pretensions. Still, it is a city of smarties. Take the brains away and we're talking Palookaville.

—Sam Allis

Boston's three major industries are sports, politics, and revenge.

—Larry Moulter

We are awfully sick of Boston. The only unconventional people here are charming screwballs, who never finish a picture or publish a line.

—Robert Lowell

A moral and intellectual nursery, always busy applying first principles to trifles.

—*George Santayana*

Everything good that ever happened to me happened because I stayed in Boston.

—*Lloyd Schwartz*

Boston is nicer & noisier than ever.

—*Louisa May Alcott*

A Boston man is the east wind made flesh.

—*Thomas Appleton*

A proper Bostonian never showed any emotion but hauteur.

—*Dorothy West*

Boston is defective, out-of-date, vain and lazy, but if you're not in a hurry, it has a deep, secret appeal.

—*Elizabeth Hardwick*

Boston would rather perish by fire and sword than to be suspected of vulgarity; a critical, fastidious, reluctant Boston, dissatisfied with the rest of the hemisphere.

—*William Dean Howells*

It is provincial; it tends to stagnate.

—*Charles Francis Adams*

The Bostonians are very well in their way. Their hotels are bad. Their pumpkin pies are delicious. Their poetry is not so good. Their Common is no common thing—and the duck-pond might answer— if its answer could be heard for the frogs.

—*Edgar Allan Poe*

You people in Boston are greedy for your traditions. I think you all have a little Ritz blood in you. That's why Boston is one of the few cities in the world that is worthy of a proper Ritz hotel.

—*Charles Ritz*

The proper Bostonian is not by nature a traveler. The Beacon Hill lady, who, chided for her lack of travel, asked simply, "Why should I travel when I'm already here?" would seem to have put the matter in a nutshell.

—*Cleveland Amory*

When you speak of the market
That's known as Faneuil,
Kindly pronounce it
To rhyme with Dan'l.

—*An Almanac for Bostonians*

In Boston, when you pass a building, you practically rub shoulders
with it—it becomes personal. When Bostonians think of the Old
State House or Faneuil Hall, they are affectionate about them.

—*Joan Goody*

My two most important buildings are in Boston.

—*Henry Cobb, architect of Pei, Cobb, Freed and Partners*

It's not hot enough, it's not crowded enough, there's not enough
asphalt, and you can see over buildings too easily.

—*Frank O'Hara*

I've been walking through the city since 1956, writing in notebooks
wherever I went. There is a sense of Boston being all around you.

—*Peter Davison*

[Boston is] a state of mind rather than a city.

—*Mark De Wolfe Howe*

My old beloved town whose very dirt is interesting to my eyes.

—*Louisa May Alcott*

I hate Boston, I don't know why. . . . The general spirit is so far, far, far back that it gets on my nerves.

—*Lincoln Steffens*

Bostonians (I am not a Bostonian) seem to have two notions of hospitality—a dinner with people you have never seen before nor never wish to see again and a drive in Mount Auburn Cemetery, where you will see the worst man can do in the way of disfiguring nature. Your memory of the dinner is expected to reconcile you to the prospect of the graveyard.

—*James Russell Lowell*

I didn't know the world contained as many negroes as I saw throng-
ing downtown Roxbury at night, especially on Saturdays. Neon
lights, nightclubs, poolhalls, bars, the cars they drove! Restaurants
made the streets smell—rich, greasy, down-home black cooking!
Juke boxes blared Erskine Hawkins, Duke Ellington, Cootie Williams,
dozens of others.

—*Malcolm X*

I hog a whole house on Boston's
"hardly passionate Marlborough Street,"
where even the man
scavenging filth in the back alley trash cans,
has two children, a beach wagon, a helpmate,
and is "a young Republican."

—*Robert Lowell*

Here I am in Boston, on Marlborough Street, number 239. I am looking out on a snowstorm. It fell like a great armistice, bringing all simple struggles to an end.

—*Elizabeth Hardwick*

Though badly outclassed in economic might and political clout . . . Boston could yet claim a kind of cultural—or even moral—supremacy. She could play Athens to New York's Rome. The result was a strange amalgam of local attitude: what might be called a superiority/inferiority complex. And from this arose a new Bostonism—a distinctive tradition of Noble Defeat. Boston would lose, repeatedly and emphatically lose, but there was grace, even elegance, in her losing.

—*John Demos*

It is simply that in Boston the custom is to keep a civil tongue even
in the company of calamities.

—*George Frazier*

It's kind of that dream city, you know? You know, *Boston*. It'd be
sweet to live there. . . . It's a rad place to live, and there's the history
and everything.

—*Jared Palomar*

You're from Boston if you could sell your house and buy a small town
in Iowa.

—*Hub humor*

The yuppies are coming. . . . What this neighborhood needs is a [expletive] crime wave to get property values back where they belong.

—*Dave Boyle, in* Mystic River

[Boston marriage is] an antique phrase, dating back to the 1800s. In Victorian times, women who wanted to maintain their independence and freedom opted out of marriage and often paired up to live together, acting as each other's "wives" and "helpmeets."

—*Pagan Kennedy*

Marriage . . . is a damnably serious business, particularly around Boston.

—*John P. Marquand*

First families in Boston have tended toward marrying each other in a way that would do justice to the planned marriages of European royalty.

—*Cleveland Amory*

South Boston is probably the most cohesive, self-conscious and proud neighborhood in the city. In many ways, it is a perfect example of what Americans mean when they speak of neighborhood.

—*Oscar Handlin*

When I got to Broadway [in South Boston] with its rows of double- and triple-parked cars, I was shocked to be once again in a place where traffic came to a grinding halt to let women with baby carriages cross the street.

—*Michael Patrick MacDonald*

There is about Boston a certain reminiscent and classical tone, suggesting an authenticity and piety which few other American cities possess.

—*E. B. White*

Dear old Boston, what an unlovely place it is!

—*George Santayana*

I could not hear of a liberated Boston lady going to bed with an unconventional Boston gentleman, without thinking: "Oh, hell! They've thought it all out." I could not imagine bed with a liberated Boston lady anyway.

—*Thomas Wolfe*

Feminism, like Boston, is a state of mind. It is the state of mind of women who realize that their whole position in the social order is antiquated, as a woman cooking over an open fire with heavy iron pots would know that her entire household was out of date.

—*Rheta Childe Dorr*

The next Augustan age will dawn on the other side of the Atlantic. There will, perhaps, be a Thucydides at Boston, a Xenophon at New York, and, in time, a Virgil at Mexico, and a Newton at Peru.

—*Horace Walpole*

A certain chronic irritability—a sort of Bostonitis—which, in its primitive Puritan forms, seemed due to knowing too much of his neighbors and thinking too much of himself.

—*Henry Adams*

The readers of the *Boston Evening Transcript*
Sway in the wind like a field of ripe corn.

—Boston Evening Transcript

Solid men of Boston, banish long potations!
Solid men of Boston, make no long orations!

—*American song*

Cold Roast Boston as lifestyle has always had much to be said for it.
Talk can be cheap, emotions misleading, sacrifice more controlling
than kindly. Undoubtedly there are some emotions so deeply held
and keenly felt that to say nothing about them is sometimes to say
everything superbly.

—*Douglass Shand-Tucci*

Boston was big and busy, a city smothering in the veins of tradition. Rows of houses melted one into another, and stout Irishwomen wore scarves over their heads and hurried in the cold, carrying milk pails to the grocery store. Intellectually, Boston was a top-and-bottom metropolis, a seat of learning and laborers; it was Harvard and Scollay Square; a port for Irish immigrants and high-stepping politicians; a place of Brahmins, bulldozers, banks, and fresh lobster.

—*Jim Bishop*

We thought we were in the best place in the world in this neighborhood, in the all-Irish housing projects where everyone claimed to be Irish even if his name was Spinnoli. . . . Southie was Boston's proud Irish neighborhood.

—*Michael Patrick MacDonald*

The Boston Irish have become people of education, culture, and refinement. To a great extent, in their prolonged struggle for survival and achievement, they did turn Boston into an Irish city.

—Thomas H. O'Connor

I sincerely believe that the public institutions and charities of Boston are as nearly perfect as the most considerable wisdom, benevolence and humanity can make them.

—Charles Dickens

Nothing quieted doubt so completely as the mental calm of the Unitarian clergy. Doubts were a waste of thought. . . . Boston had solved the universe; or had offered and realised the best solution yet tried.

—Henry Adams

The Puritanical idea of uplift ever lingers in the blood of the descendants of the first colonists of Massachusetts Bay. It may be true that occasionally they are shortsighted and oblivious to certain faults in their surroundings which may be obvious to others, but when their attention is directed toward these faults, they leave no stone unturned in an effort at rectification.

—John P. Marquand

Boston was fractured and knit and fractured again over women's rights, Graham's dietary innovations, the organization of the fire department, Sunday mail delivery, and, always, slavery.

—Martha Saxton

Boston all too often displayed a mean and selfish spirit that belied its reputation as the Cradle of Liberty and the Athens of America. . . . Whether it was political intolerance against those who protested the Puritan establishment in the eighteenth century, religious bigotry against Roman Catholics in the nineteenth century, or displays of racial hatred against African Americans in the twentieth century, Boston was capable of frequently disillusioning even those friends who most admired it.

—*Thomas H. O'Connor*

I was just a little girl from Boston, a place of dull people with funny accents.

—*Dorothy West*

It is a great pleasure to come back to a city where my accent is considered normal and where they pronounce the words the way they are spelled!

—*John F. Kennedy*

I was born on A Street, raised up on B Street,
Southie is my home town. There's something about it,
Permit me to shout it, we're tough from miles around.
We have doctors and trappers, preachers and flappers
And men from old County Down.
Say they'll take you and break you but never forsake you—
Southie is my home town.

—*traditional song*

South Boston, a peninsula that was once a cow pasture known as
Dorchester Heights . . . was separated entirely from downtown
Boston and the world-apart mentality persists to this day. It is still a
place where loyalty is a lifelong thing and outsiders have to prove
themselves slowly over time.

—*Boston Globe Spotlight Team*

It takes no degree in sociology to say that a Southie, confronted by
a punk poking a finger into his eye, most often will respond with a
straight right.

—*Dave Kindred*

I saw the sky descending, black and white,
Not blue, on Boston.

—*Robert Lowell*

We bank over Boston. I am safe. I put on my hat.
I am almost someone going home. The story has
ended.

—*Anne Sexton*

Boston is a kind of Rome. Only colder.

—*Andrei Codrescu*

The "hub" is the core. It remains stationary, yet it is the center of change. Think of Boston as that city that remains as the core. Core qualities don't change easily.

—*Thomas H. O'Connor*

The Bostonian who leaves Boston ought to be condemned to perpetual exile.

—*William Dean Howells*

III

SHOT HEARD 'ROUND THE WORLD

Massachusetts in the Revolution

It is a State of tradition, but part of its tradition is its history of revolt.
—WPA Guide to Massachusetts

Liberty is the proper end and object of authority, and cannot subsist without it; and it is liberty to that which is good, just, and honest.
—*John Winthrop*

It was impossible to beat the notion of liberty out of the people as it was rooted in them from their childhood.
—*Thomas Gage, commander in chief of the British Army in America*

There is danger from all men. The only maxim of a free government
ought to be to trust no man living with power to endanger the
public liberty.

—John Adams

By the sword we seek peace, but peace only under liberty.

—Massachusetts state motto

We may all be soon under the necessity of keeping shooting irons.

—Samuel Adams

The colonists are by the law of nature free born, as indeed all men are, white or black. . . . It is a clear truth that those who every day barter away other men's liberty will soon care little for their own.

—*James Otis*

I wish this cursed place [Boston] was burned.

—*Thomas Gage, commander in chief of the British Army in America*

We threw a parcel of shells, and the whole town [Boston] was instantly in flames.

—*British general John Burgoyne*

The American Revolution was a remarkably successful revolution. . . .
It was also, as revolutions go, extremely unromantic. The radicals,
the real revolutionaries, were middle-class Massachusetts merchants
with commercial interests, and their revolution was about the right
to make money.

—*Mark Kurlansky*

Rally, Mohawks!
Bring out your axes,
And tell King George we'll pay no taxes
On his foreign tea . . .

—*The Rallying of the Tea Party*

No taxation without representation

—*Reverend Jonathan Mayhew*

Taxation without representation is tyranny.

—*James Otis*

"No taxation without representation!" galvanized the populace and marked the birth of a great American political tradition: the reductionist rhyming chant.

—The Daily Show with Jon Stewart Presents America (The Book) *by Jon Stewart, Ben Karlin, and David Javerbaum*

[W]e the subscribers do strictly [agree] that we will totally abstain from the use of tea (sickness excepted), not only in our respective families, but that we will absolutely refuse it, if it should be offered to us on any occasion whatsoever. . . .

—*Boston "ladies of the highest rank and influence"*

Who knows how tea will mingle with saltwater?

—*Samuel Adams*

I must be weaned [of tea], and the sooner the better.

—*John Adams*

The scituation of this town is truly deplorable and its future prospects really distressing to every mind susceptible of the feelings of humanity . . . under the protection of General Gage we shall be able to speak our minds freely, and open the eyes of a deluded people, who have hitherto been deceiv'd by a sett of designing villains and bankrupts. . . .

—*Loyalist Richard Lechmere*

To a degree, academic freedom is a reality today because Socrates practiced civil disobedience. In our own nation, the Boston Tea Party represented a massive act of civil disobedience.

—*Martin Luther King, Jr.*

And so, on a cold December night, a party of Bostonians dressed as Mohawk Indians boarded ships anchored in the harbor and dumped thousands of pounds of tea into the Atlantic. . . . British authorities immediately closed the harbor and clamped down on the Massachusetts government, a move brewer/patriot Samuel Adams called "wicked retahded" in Ye Boston Globe.

—The Daily Show with Jon Stewart Presents America (The Book) *by Jon Stewart, Ben Karlin, and David Javerbaum*

The troubles and difficulties the town is thrown into by the Tea affair has lessen'd the value of real estates accordingly.

—Loyalist Richard Lechmere

The hellish crew fell upon my house with the rage of devils.

—British lieutenant governor Thomas Hutchinson

The Dye is cast: The People have passed the River and cutt away the Bridge.

—Samuel Adams

HERE WERE HELD THE
TOWN-MEETINGS THAT
USHERED IN THE REVOLUTION
HERE SAMUEL ADAMS, JAMES OTIS
AND JOSEPH WARREN EXHORTED
HERE THE MEN OF BOSTON PROVED
THEMSELVES INDEPENDENT
COURAGEOUS FREEMEN
WORTHY TO RAISE ISSUES
WHICH WERE TO CONCERN THE
LIBERTY AND HAPPINESS
OF MILLIONS YET UNBORN

—entrance sign at Old South Meeting House, Boston

The spacious Old South Meeting House taken possession of by the Light Horse 17th Regiment of [British] Dragoons commanded by Lieutenant Colonel Samuel Birch. The pulpit, pews, and seats all cut to pieces and carried off in the most savage manner as can be expressed, and destined for a riding school.

—Timothy Newell

The saving of the Old South Meeting House is worth remembering as the first instance in Boston where respect for the historical and architectural heritage of the city triumphed over considerations of profit, expediency, laziness and vulgar convenience.

—Walter Muir Whitehill

America is a mere bully, from one end to the other, and the Bostonians by far the greatest bullies.

—Thomas Gage, commander in chief of the British Army in America

If I draw my sword but half out of my scabbard, the whole banditti of Massachusetts will run away.

—Major John Pitcairn of the Royal Marines

Whoever dares to look upon them as an irregular mob, will find himself much mistaken. They have men amongst them who know very well what they are about.

—*Brigadier Lord Hugh Percy*

I set off upon a very good Horse; it was then about 11 o'Clock, and very pleasant. After I had passed Charlestown Neck . . . I saw two men on Horse back under a Tree. When I got near them, I discovered they were British officer. One tryed to git a head of Me, and the other to take me. I turned my Horse very quick and Galloped towards Charlestown neck, and then pushed for the Medford Road. . . . In Medford, I awaked the Captain of the Minute men; and after that, I alarmed almost every house, till I got to Lexington.

—*Paul Revere*

Paul Revere?
Ain't he the Yankee who had to go for help?

—*old Texas joke*

Listen, my children, and you shall hear
Of the midnight ride of Paul Revere,
On the eighteenth of April, in Seventy-five;
Hardly a man is now alive
Who remembers that famous day and year.
He said to his friend, "If the British march
By land or sea from the town to-night,
Hang a lantern aloft in the belfry arch
Of the North Church tower as a signal light, —
One, if by land, and two, if by sea;
And I on the opposite shore will be,
Ready to ride and spread the alarm
Through every Middlesex village and farm,
For the country folk to be up and to arm."

—*Henry Wadsworth Longfellow*

In American museums, Paul Revere spurs are as numerous as fragments of the True Cross.

—*David Hackett Fischer*

To understand how the world has changed, think back to the warm and fuzzy telephone ads that once encouraged us to reach out and touch someone. Compare that to my favorite telephone ad of this season. It features Paul Revere in his full midnight ride regalia trying to reach John Adams, who is, of course, screening his calls: "John, John, this is Paul. Pick up. It's important."

—*Ellen Goodman*

'Tis all very well for the children to hear
Of the midnight ride of Paul Revere;
But why should my name be quite forgot,
Who rode as boldly and well, God wot?
Why should I ask? The reason is clear—
My name was Dawes and his Revere.

—*Helen F. Moore*

It was two by the village clock
When his inner tube gave a hiss.
He felt the car come down with a shock,
He jacked, and pried, and pumped, and said,
"I wish I'd come on a horse instead."

—*Two Long Fellows*

The first stroke will decide a good deal.
—*Thomas Gage, commander in chief of the British Army in America,*
referring to meeting rebels in the first military encounter

Lay down your arms, you damned rebels, and disperse!
—*British Major John Pitcairn*

Stand your ground. Don't fire unless fired upon. But if they mean to
have a war, let it begin here.
—*Captain John Parker*

Fire, fellow soldiers! For God's sake fire!
—*Colonial Major John Buttrick*

Stand your ground. . . . Your cause is just and God will bless you!
—*Concord minister William Emerson*

By the rude bridge that arched the flood,
Their flag to April's breeze unfurled,
Here once the embattled farmers stood,
and fired the shot heard 'round the world.
—*Ralph Waldo Emerson*

I mean this is a glorious day for America.

—*Samuel Adams*

The Die is Cast . . . The Sword is now our only yet dreadful alternative.

—*Abigail Adams*

Here there is glory for all. The National Park will unite Lexington, Lincoln, and Concord in a memorial to the first effective stand against Colonial rule, a revolution still going on in other parts of the world.

—*Concord Journal*

But the emotional heart of Revolutionary Concord is the North Bridge. One million tourists walk across it every year. . . . I sat by the bridge and took pleasure in its pastoral calm. It wasn't the first time I had been struck by the tendency of America's old battlefields to be places of unusual tranquillity.

—*William Zinsser*

I shall enter on no encomium upon Massachusetts; she needs none. There she is. Behold her, and judge for yourselves. There is her history; the world knows it by heart. The past, at least, is secure. There is Boston and Concord and Lexington and Bunker Hill; and there they will remain forever.

—*Daniel Webster*

To all friends of American Liberty, be it known that this morning before breake of day a brigade consisting of 1000 or 1200 men landed at Phip's Farm at Cambridge & marched to Lexington where they found a company of our colony militia in arms, upon whom they fired without any provocation and killed 6 men and wounded 4 others.

—*Lexington Alarm*

This evening intelligence hath been receiv'd, that about 1200 of the regular troops, have proceeded from Boston toward Concord; and having fired on the inhabitants, and killed a number of them, at Lexington, are now actually engaged in butchering and destroying our brethren in the most inhuman manner. The inhabitants opposed them with zeal and courage, and numbers have already fallen on both sides.

—Stephen Hopkins

Amid all the terrors of battle I was so busily engaged in Harvard Library that I never even heard of . . . [it] until it was completed.

—Harvard scholar

One can join for the simple pleasure of dressing funny, waving at neighbors in parades and sharing a beer at the tavern. . . . The main thing though is having a love and deep respect for our history. What we accomplished in obtaining our independence remains awe-inspiring and should never be forgotten.

—Kevin Gatlin, Sudbury Militia reenactor

During the whole of the march from Lexington the rebels kept an incessant irregular fire from all points at the column. . . . Our men had very few opportunities of getting good shots at the rebels, as they hardly ever fired but under cover of a stone wall, from behind a tree, or out of a house. . . . In the road, indeed, in our rear, they were most numerous and came on pretty close, frequently calling out "King Hancock forever!"

—*British lieutenant Frederick MacKenzie*

One of our most bawling demagogues and voluminous writers is a crazy doctor.

—*Tory pamphleteer, referring to Dr. Joseph Warren*

The decisive day is come.

—*Bunker Hill rallying cry*

Don't fire until you see the whites of their eyes.

—*Colonial colonel William Prescott*

[T]he God of armies will teach their hand to war and their fingers to fight.

—*Reverend Thomas Allen of Stockbridge before the Battle of Bennington*

We therefore, the people of Massachusetts, acknowledging with grateful hearts, the goodness of the Great Legislator of the Universe, in affording us, in the course of His Providence, an opportunity, deliberately and peaceably, without fraud, violence or surprize, on entering into an Original, explicit, and Solemn Compact with each other; and of forming a new Constitution of Civil Government, for Ourselves and Posterity, and devoutly imploring His direction in so interesting a design, DO agree upon, ordain and establish, the following Declaration of Rights, and Frame of Government, as the CONSTITUTION OF THE COMMONWEALTH OF MASSACHUSETTS.

—*Preamble to the Constitution of the Commonwealth,* 1780

May the principles of our excellent Constitution, founded in Nature and in the Rights of Man, be ably defended here: And may the same principles be deeply engraven in the hearts of all citizens.

—*Governor Samuel Adams*

All hail to Massachusetts, the land of the free and the brave!
For Bunker Hill and Charlestown, and flag we love to wave;
For Lexington and Concord, and the shot heard 'round the world;
All hail to Massachusetts, we'll keep her flag unfurled.
She stands upright for freedom's light that shines from sea to sea;
All hail to Massachusetts! Our country 'tis of thee!
  —*Official Song of the Commonwealth, by Arthur J. Marsh*

Independence forever.
  —*John Adams's last words*

IV

A WONDERFUL
PLACE TO
GROW UP

Massachusetts Cities and Towns

Only a Massachusetts native knows how to pronounce towns like
Worcester, Eastham, Chatham, Haverhill, Peabody, Scituate,
Leominster or Gloucester.

—Bay State humor

There was an artist's shadow beside every cow in Gloucester, and the
cows themselves were dying from eating paint rags.

—John Sloan

There are houses in Gloucester where grooves have been worn into
the floorboards by women pacing past an upstairs window, looking
out to sea.

—Sebastian Junger

Gloucester . . . is a rough, downhill fishing town. Fine old wooden merchant's houses view the sea from up on the hills, while nineteenth- and twentieth-century brick buildings—the look of old blue-collar New England—dominate the lower part of town around a well-sheltered and busy waterfront.

—Mark Kurlansky

There is probably no individual beyond Gloucester whose parentage may not be referred to a particular set of people, at a particular date in English history. It has great wealth of granite and fish. It is composed of granite; and almost its only visitors are fish.

—Harriet Martineau

Main Street, in fact, like all the rest of Gloucester, is governed by the sea. Its ancient buildings talk sea talk, informing you in signs that have swung in the wind these many years that the Marine Society meets here, that this is a place sailors will find attractive, that ship's stores are to be procured here, and sails over there.

Hildegarde Hawthorne

The bell towers are one of the highest points in Gloucester and can be seen for miles by incoming ships. Between the towers is a sculpture of the Virgin Mary, who gazes down with love and concern at a bundle in her arms. This is the Virgin who has been charged with the safety of the local fishermen. The bundle in her arms is not the infant Jesus; it's a Gloucester schooner.

—Sebastian Junger

[Cape Ann] is a singular region. If a little orchard plot is seen, here and there, it seems rescued by some chance from being grown over with granite. . . . The granite rises straight behind a house, encroaches on each side, and overhangs the roof, leaving space only for a sprinkling of grass about the door, for a red shrub or two to wave from a crevice, and a drip of water to flow down among gay weeds.

—*Harriet Martineau*

High Street from end to end is remarkable for charm and dignity, even among these old towns so given to fine streets. One splendid house, built by the sturdy sea-captains and traders of Newburyport's heyday, follows another, with old churches dominating them, great trees sheltering them.

—*Hildegarde Hawthorne*

Carriage Center of the World

—Amesbury nickname

We children felt at once that we belonged to [Beverly], as we did
to our father or our mother. The sea was its nearest neighbor, and
penetrated to every fireside, claiming close intimacy with every
home and heart. The farmers up and down the shore were as much
fishermen as farmers; they were as familiar with the Grand Banks
of Newfoundland as they were with their own potato-fields.

—Lucy Larcom

There was no worse insult in the experience of a Beverly male than
to be called a landlubber.

—Hildegarde Hawthorne

If Shillington gave me life, Ipswich was where I took possession of it, the place where in my own sense of myself I ceased to be a radically defective person.

—*John Updike*

When two Marbleheaders meet, they say to each other, "Down Bucket!" or else they say "To hell I pitch it!" Why they say it, or how they began, the Marbleheaders themselves can't tell you.

—*Josef Berger*

Almost all the old houses [in Marblehead] still stick to their rocks, and the streets are the same; were the dead in Burial Hill to clamber out of the rocky niches where they sleep within sound of the sea they loved, they would have little trouble finding their old homes.

—*Hildegarde Hawthorne*

If you wish to catch the atmosphere of the Federalist era in Massachusetts go to Salem and visit the Peabody Essex Museum with its ship-portraits. . . . Then walk up Chestnut Street and catch the sense of proportion that architects learn in a maritime community. Think of the owner scanning the harbor entrance from the roof of his house for the ship that will make his fortune or ruin him utterly.
—*George Caspar Homans and Samuel Eliot Morison*

New England has always been fabled for its eccentrics, and Salem's witch history naturally began to attract religious iconoclasts. . . . Wiccans began relocating to Boston's north shore, attracted by the "Salem" mystique and hoping for a tolerant environment.
—*David J. Skal*

I did it every witch way in Salem.
—*T-shirt*

Salem, Massachusetts, not only symbolizes witchcraft to tourists
with a casual historical interest, but is the national headquarters of
an organized, politically active and profitable cult.

—*Jay Rogers*

Massachusetts is my favorite haunt.

—*Salem bumper sticker*

Witches know how to spell.

—*Salem T-shirt*

My other car is a broom.

—*Salem bumper sticker*

Accused witches in New England were subjected to grueling ordeals, but perhaps none so challenging as locating a parking space in modern Salem during a typical October weekend.

—David J. Skal

Some day [Lowell] will put up a statue of me. And I'll even pose naked for it if they want.

—Jack Kerouac

From the beginning, Lowell had a high reputation for good order, morality, piety, and all that was dear to the old-fashioned New Englander's heart.

—Lucy Larcom

And how sinfully flattering to Lowell, this picture of her suddenly as
one of those femme fatale cities, a kind of Massachusetts Macao, with
her faster music and stronger wine luring men to inevitable doom.
— *"Pertinax," pen name of Mary Sampas at the* Lowell Sun

To me at first ["beat"] meant being poor and sleeping in subways . . .
and yet being illuminated. . . . Then I went to Lowell, Massachusetts,
in 1954. Got a room in Skid Row near the depot. Walked twenty
miles around Lowell every day. Went to my old church where I got
my first confirmation. Knelt, all alone, all alone in the church, in the
great silence of the church. . . . And I suddenly realized, beat means
beatitude! Beatific!

— *Jack Kerouac*

The very river that moves the machinery in the [Lowell] mills . . .
seems to acquire a new character from the fresh buildings of bright
red brick and painted wood among which it takes its course; and
to be as light-headed, thoughtless, and brisk a young river, in its
murmurings and tumblings, as one would desire to see.

—*Charles Dickens*

Lowell, of course, turned out to be an ugly, ratchety mill town in
unplanned sprawl along the Merrimack: shuttered factories, rail
yards blown with hapless papers, unpainted wooden buildings with
their date-plaques blurred by weather over the doors, and the tur-
reted town hall with the library next to it where Jack [Kerouac] had
read his Balzac when he was a polite, bow-tied, moody youth.

—*John Clellon Holmes*

A golden Byzantine dome rises from the roofs along the canal; a Gothic copy of Chartres rises from the slums of Moody Street; little children speak French, Greek, Polish, and even Portuguese on their way to school. And I have a recurrent dream of simply walking around the deserted twilight streets of Lowell in the mist, eager to turn every known and fabled corner . . . it always makes me happy when I wake up.

—*Jack Kerouac*

I shall be born when and where I want and I do not choose to be born at Lowell.

—*James Abbott McNeill Whistler*

City of Shoes

—*Lynn nickname*

Lynn, Lynn, city of sin!
You can't get out
but y'can always get in!

—rope-skipping rhyme

One of the wonderful things about Revere, as with some other communities that have so many ethnic groups and so many immigrant groups . . . is that yes, there's tension, and people have to kind of dance around a little bit and spar and box, and hopefully not worse than that, but hopefully they end up getting together and they have wonderful tales about one another.

—Alan Lupo

Andover was a wonderful place to grow up—just an ideal American town that never lost its innocence. People got excited over the littlest things. Your best friend would call up with incredible news like "Oh, man, one of those new Corvettes just drove by!" And you'd be devastated—screaming *No! No!* —because you missed this cataclysmic event.

—Jay Leno

Boston's Left Bank

—Cambridge nickname

I was born in East Cambridge, Massachusetts (yes, Our Fair City). I spent most of my "formative years," as they say, on Harding Street. This was just the greatest neighborhood on the planet. Kids everywhere. Just hangin' out. Nothing much happened. Just good times.

—Tom Magliozzi

Say the worst of it, Cambridge speaks English, words are given a fighting chance to speak.

—*Robert Lowell*

We live in a lovely town because everyone is doing something.

—*Julia Child, on Cambridge*

Why, if all the creative energy expended in Cambridge on paying telephone bills, signing documents, finding a cab, buying a milk-shake, bitching at the landlord and shoplifting from the Harvard Coop could be channeled into writing, playing, loving, and working, the results would probably be stupendous.

—*Raymond Mungo*

I think I've programmed myself to like the chaos. Genteel it ain't.
—*Margo Howard, on Harvard Square*

I especially miss Harvard Square—it's so unique. Nowhere else in the world will you find a man with a turban wearing a Red Sox jacket and working in a lesbian bookstore. Hey, I'm just glad my dad's working.
—*Conan O'Brien*

The Cambridge ladies who live in furnished souls
are unbeautiful and have comfortable minds.

—*e.e. cummings*

The People's Republic

—*Cambridge nickname*

[A]fter a year we moved to Wayland, Massachusetts, in the western suburbs of Boston. We lived there for maybe three years, the highlight of my childhood. We had a great neighborhood. I could ride my bike all over the place. . . . It was classic fifties suburbia with the grill on the backyard patio and *South Pacific, My Fair Lady Lady*, and Harry Belafonte on the big hi-fi speaker in the living room.

—*Tom Hamilton*

All those American Lit courses . . . were grounded in the intellect of writers who lived in Concord: Ralph Waldo Emerson and Henry David Thoreau, Nathaniel Hawthorne and Margaret Fuller, Bronson and Louisa May Alcott. To judge from their turn of mind, living in Concord bred an almost holy belief in individual freedom . . . those Concord writers were no less American Revolutionaries than the townsmen who asserted their resistance in 1775. . . .

—William Zinsser

Concord is one of New England's loveliest examples of collaboration between nature and man. The white homes and churches sit on flat lawns that gracefully evolve from back yards into wide meadows. These undulating fields edge the placid Concord River. . . . The river grows yellow water lilies, and along the shores stand silvery green reeds, bullrushes, cattails, and golden pickerel weed.

—Martha Saxton

This is our lake country.

—Henry David Thoreau, on Concord

With a population of slightly over two thousand, Concord had perhaps a higher percentage of concerned and articulate inhabitants than any other small town in America.

—Paul Brooks

I think we escape something by living in the villages. In Concord here there is some milk of life, we are not so raving distracted with wind and dyspepsia. The mania takes a milder form. People go a-fishing, and know the taste of their meat. They cut their own whippletree in the woodlot, they know something practically of the sun and the east wind, of the underpinning and the roofing of the house, of the pan and the mixture of soils.

—Ralph Waldo Emerson

Emerson was the town's most sustaining figure, and through him Concord became characterized by a noble, vague, romantic transcendentalism. It was the home of American idealism, and although many found it gloomy and cold . . . nevertheless it was unique in the attempts of a disproportionate number of its citizens to lead exemplary lives.

—*Martha Saxton*

Poor dull Concord. Nothing colorful has come through here since the Redcoats.

—*Louisa May Alcott*

Those who gave the town its name might have chosen differently if they could have read the future.

—*John T. Faris, on Concord*

Most men are apt to exaggerate the merits of their birthplace. . . .
But there never was in the world a better example of a pure and
beautiful democracy, in the highest sense of the term, than the
town of Concord from 1826 to the close of the war. If there were
any aristocracy, it was an aristocracy of personal worth.

—*George Frisbie Hoar*

I have traveled a good deal in Concord and everywhere, in shops,
and offices, and fields, the inhabitants have appeared to me to be
doing penance in a thousand remarkable ways.

—*Henry David Thoreau*

There was a young lady from Concord
Who became so completely bonkered
She tried to pronounce Thoreau
In the accepted way, you know
But the accent it couldn't be conquered.

—*John Garrison*

Watch City

—*Waltham nickname*

Quincy . . . was one of the landing-places of Captain John Smith in 1614. On his map he called the place London, for, though there was no town there, he felt sure it would one day be the scene of a great settlement. His map was, in a sense, prophetic, for, while a metropolis did not spring up there . . . John Hancock was born in the neighborhood, and so were two presidents of the United States, John Adams and John Quincy Adams.

—John T. Faris

Birthplace of the American Dream

—Quincy nickname

Kilroy was here.

—James Kilroy's rivet-check markings at Quincy's Bethlehem Steel Shipyard

Scituate, The Irish Riviera

—T-shirt

America's Hometown

—Plymouth nickname

In New Bedford, fathers, they say, give whales for dowers to their daughters, and portion off their nieces with a few porpoises a piece.
—Herman Melville

On the wharves of New Bedford I received my first light. I saw there industry without bustle, labor without noise, toil—honest, earnest, and exhaustive—without the whip.

—*Frederick Douglass*

[N]owhere in America will you find more patrician-like houses; parks and gardens more opulent, than in New Bedford. . . . Yes; all these brave houses and flowery gardens came from the Atlantic, Pacific, and Indian oceans. One and all, they were harpooned and dragged up hither from the bottom of the sea.

—*Herman Melville*

Once lined with world wandering whaleships, today the docks of
New Bedford are home to hundreds of commercial fishing vessels.
The fleet, made up of mostly groundfishing boats (draggers) and
scallopers, has consistently made New Bedford the number one
fishing port in the country in terms of the dollar value of its catch.
                    —*New Bedford Whaling National Historical Park*

In this same New Bedford there stands a Whaleman's Chapel, and
few are the moody fishermen, shortly bound for the Indian Ocean
or Pacific, who fail to make a Sunday visit to the spot.
                                        —*Herman Melville*

Living long is so much the practice here that people say "it must be something in the climate"—though one spry octogenarian has confided to me that "it's only because it takes such an eternal long time to convince a Cape Cod Yankee of anything."

—*Josef Berger*

It made the Summer People over in its own image of peculiarity and individualism. It encouraged them to be themselves. [Cape Cod] said, in effect, We've told the rest of America to go to Hell for three hundred years. Go thou and do likewise. We don't care a damn what you do.

—*Jonathan Norton Leonard*

The Cape Cod girls they have no combs,
They comb their hair with codfish bones;
The Cape Cod boys they have no sleds,
They slide downhill on codfish heads.

—traditional sea shanty

You're from Massachusetts if you've spent a summer hanging out on the Cape.

—Bay State humor

Bars on the Cape are scarcer than you would suppose. In some of the best hotels guests can practically choke to death.

—Eleanor Early

Without the C it's just od

—*Cape Cod T-shirt*

The "antique belt" extends from Chatham to Hyannis, with many other shops dotting the Cape. . . . [B]ear in mind that the measurements of the *Mayflower* on record [are] 90 feet from stem to stern and 20 feet in the beam, with a depth hold of 11 to 14 feet, and that enough objects have already been established in this country as genuine *Mayflower* cargo to fill a warehouse of a hundred times this cubic area.

—*Josef Berger*

Let's jump into the car, honey,
and head straight for the Cape,
where the cock on our housetop crows
that the weather's fair,
and my garden waits for me
to coax it into bloom.

—*Stanley Kunitz*

I had a large house [in Barnstable] with lots of kids in it—three
of my own and three adopted. And Cape Cod was a padded cell
where children couldn't possibly hurt themselves when they were
growing up.

—*Kurt Vonnegut*

The time President Kennedy spent in Hyannisport during his youth
and his presidency were among the happiest days of his life.

—*Edward M. Kennedy*

There are no braggarts at the tip of the Cape. Folks there have a horror of letting the tongue's reach exceed its grasp. Before delivering any statement they weigh it with care and then cut off a large piece, much as the butcher cuts the bone out of a steak.

—*Robert Haven Schauffler*

No other spot on the Cape is richer in folklore and piquant legend than Truro. Here was the famous Lyars' Bench, utilized for the sole purpose of telling tall stories.

—WPA Guide to Massachusetts

Provincetown lives at a bemused distance from the rest of the country. It does not quite consider itself American, and in this regard it is probably more right than wrong.

—*Michael Cunningham*

Free living to the hilt, Provincetown may delight or offend, but it cannot be ignored. It grasps at all who come here, asserting gaudiness and serenity, creative independence and a passion for the inane.

—*Tom Melham*

These dunes are the arch enemies of the town. They are forever changing, forever new, forever advancing to bury Provincetown in their dry lava much as Vesuvius buried Herculaneum.

—*Robert Haven Schauffler*

The Pilgrim Monument, Provincetown's outstanding landmark for travelers by land, sea and air, is thoroughly American in its makeup. Although the Pilgrims had never been to Italy, the design is Italian; the plans were made by an army engineer of French and Swiss descent; it was built by the Irish and is taken care of by the Portuguese; and annually it is climbed by several thousand *Mayflower* descendants.

—*Josef Berger*

This was the '70s, remember, so factor that in when you conjure up the image of a once quaint New England port town, clogged with tourists, daytrippers, hippies, drifters, lobster poachers, slutty chicks, dopers, refugees from Key West, and thousands upon thousands of energetically cruising gay men. For a rootless young man with sensualist inclinations, [Provincetown] was the perfect getaway.

—*Anthony Bourdain*

It is considered a truism in Provincetown that gay men go to the beach with Speedos and a towel, while lesbians take as much as they can carry.

—*Michael Cunningham*

Three miles long and two streets wide, [Provincetown] curls around the bay . . . a gaudy run with Mediterranean splashes of color, crowded steep-pitched roofs, fishing piers and fishing boats whose stench of mackerel and gasoline is as aphrodisiac to the sensuous nose as the clean bar-whisky smell of a nightclub where call girls congregate.

—*Norman Mailer*

Just as the Chinese date their history from the dynasties of their emperors, so Provincetown dates hers from the great storms that have proved particularly destructive and terrible.

—*Hildegarde Hawthorne*

The main street [of Provincetown], especially in the moon's limelight, is almost too good and unrealistic to be true. The theatrical way which the houses occasionally have of jutting their upper stories out toward the opposite neighbor is pleasant to eyes fresh from metropolitan brownstone fronts. They remind one of old salts, perched on coils of rope and almost bumping foreheads in order to swap yarns.

—Robert Haven Schauffler

Provincetown is, has always been, an eccentrics' sanctuary, more or less the way other places are bird sanctuaries or wild game preserves. It is the only small town I know of where those who live unconventionally seem to outnumber those who live within the prescribed boundaries of home and licensed marriage, respectable job and biological children.

—Michael Cunningham

One of the first things that strikes me when I cross the Sagamore
Bridge onto the Mid-Cape Highway is how unsexy the Cape is.
I mean that as a compliment. There's no drama in the air, no desire,
qualities that, along with a contaminating tension and covetousness,
suffuse the South Fork on Long Island (and, increasingly, Martha's
Vineyard).

—*Paul Theroux*

It was in Martha's Vineyard that I really began to mature my painting—
to get a grip on my emerging style and way of doing things. I painted
the landscape there and the old people. About the old Yankees of
the island there was something deeply appealing. Many of them,
for all their crotchety ways, had the nobility of medieval saints.

—*Thomas Hart Benton*

Back in those days [of family vacations on Martha's Vineyard], it wasn't a string of McMansions and jets idling at the airport waiting to take the investment bankers to Long Island. It was a cheap place to go spend a summer, an outpost with really interesting people.

—*James Taylor*

The best times I've had in my life have been right here [on Martha's Vineyard].

—*Carly Simon*

Martha's Vineyard
Always room for one more bloom

—*T-shirt*

My plan was to leave the earth. And then I thought, to hell with it, I'll go to the Vineyard.

*—humorist Art Buchwald,
on decision to leave hospice care in summer 2006*

I find it a lot healthier for me to be [on Martha's Vineyard] where I can go outside in my bare feet. In ways, it reminds me a little bit of a certain kind of atmosphere that was in the mental hospital I spent time in.

—James Taylor

America's dissidents are not committed to mental hospitals and sent into exile; they thrive and prosper and buy a house on Nantucket and take flyers in the commodities market.

—Ted Turner

People in Nantucket invest their money in whaling vessels, the same way that you do yours in approved state stocks bringing in good interest.

—Herman Melville

The beauty of Nantucket town, which has been repeatedly knocked about by destiny, is essentially sturdy. Its homes range from mere shingled cabins to town houses of opulent splendour, but they are nearly all tough and self-reliant structures—island structures, in fact. Reliability rather than grace is their hallmark, and they stand there, street after street, in attitudes of neighbourly but hardly gushing resolution.

—Jan Morris

Living on an island that was almost the same distance from the
mainland as England was from France, Nantucketers developed
a British sense of themselves as a distinct and superior people,
privileged citizens of what Ralph Waldo Emerson called the "Nation
of Nantucket."

—*Nathaniel Philbrick*

One wonders sometimes if the powers that be on Nantucket don't
regard the Constitution as just another bit of Federalism, or the
Supreme Court as nothing more than a bunch of off-islanders who
can't be expected to understand.

—*Frank Conroy*

Nantucket is truly a community knit together by its own culture and traditions. The universal motivation is to get along with each other as best we can—and to go to the beach (or out on the water) as often as possible.

—Elaine Katz

We have something to sell; that something is health, comfort and pleasure.

—Nantucket Inquirer and Mirror

There are persons here who, if they don't douse your chili with catsup, express their hostility in more devious ways, like, for instance, inviting you to their parties.

—George Frazier, on Nantucket

Nantucket public manners incline to the offhand, edging away sometimes into the surly. Service is by no means always with a smile. Being of charitable disposition, I attribute this to historical osmosis, and like to think it just another symptom of Nantucket's ornery island pride—part of this citizenry's stubborn resistance to everything that might taint or trivialize their island.

—*Jan Morris*

Many of the true pleasures of Nantucket are not easily gained and cannot be purchased on demand . . . they have to be like everything else in life, earned.

—*David Halberstam*

But let those who are unwilling to become slaves of the island, keep safely away from it. If they climb the streets of Nantucket, the old whaling town; walk out two miles to the tablet that marks the birth-place of Abiah Folger, mother of Benjamin Franklin; stroll on to Siasconset; remain there long enough to call it 'Sconset; then pass on to Sankaty Head, eighty-five feet above the sea, and look toward far-away Europe, it is almost a certainty that they will be Nantucket converts for life.

—*John T. Faris*

I like the Acacia trees that remind me of Africa. I like the quiet call of Sconset on a weekday. I like the sound of the tides, the fog. People don't blow their horns up here as much as they do everywhere else. There is more niceness up here. I hope it doesn't get too big-city. Crowds don't bother me per se. It's when they get pushy. I don't want Nantucket to get pushy.

—*Chris Matthews*

It's nicer on Nantucket

—bumper sticker

little grey lady of the sea

—whalers' nickname for Nantucket

Nantucket really is islandness epitomized. . . . Its natives are extremely proud of being different. They feed upon their own extraordinary circumstances, long since flavoured by rich additives of legend and anecdote, and they are engaged now as always in an interminable battle to keep Nantucket as thoroughly Nantuckety as it possibly can be.

—Jan Morris

Where else but from Nantucket did those aboriginal whalemen, the Red-Men, first sally out in canoes to give chase to the Leviathan? And where but from Nantucket, too, did that first adventurous little sloop put forth, partly laden with imported cobblestones—so goes the story—to throw at the whales, in order to discover when they were nigh enough to risk a harpoon from the bowsprit.

—Herman Melville

Nantucket is not typically American, concerned with its large treasures like the Grand Canyon, the redwoods, the Mississippi, or the deserts and mountains. Nantucket is in the realm of the small.

—Frank Conroy

Nantucket was a town of roof dwellers. Nearly every house, its shingles painted red or left to weather into gray, had a roof-mounted platform known as a walk. While its intended use was to facilitate putting out chimney fires with buckets of sand, the walk was also an excellent place to look out to sea with a spyglass, to search for the sails of returning ships.

—Nathaniel Philbrick

There was an old man from Nantucket
Who kept all his cash in a bucket
His daughter, named Nan,
Ran away with a man
And as for the bucket, Nantucket.

—traditional

I am the Man from Nantucket

—T-shirt

My love for astronomy was born on that island . . . the spirit of the place had also much to do with my pursuit. In Nantucket people quite generally were in the habit of observing the heavens, and a sextant was to be found in almost every house.

—Maria Mitchell

Everyone should have a Nantucket

—bumper sticker

Chair City of the World
—*Gardner slogan in honor of its proud history of furniture making*

May we realize that the true greatness of Worcester is not evidenced now and never will be evidenced by the number and length of its streets, its magnificent buildings, its extensive factories, or its great population, but it is found now, and ever will be found, if found at all, in the minds and hearts of the people.

—*Burton W. Potter*

The Heart of the Commonwealth

—*Worcester motto*

Never order poor goods in Worcester County. They are not
made here.

—Worcester Board of Trade

The Shredded Wheat Capital of the World

—Late nineteenth-century nickname for Worcester

It's Wustah

—Worcester T-shirt

People in the field of public health believed that [three-decker] buildings did much to account for the general good health of Worcester's populations. Each apartment received sunshine and fresh air from all sides. People, young and old, took their daily airings on the comfortable porches, where they could enjoy some of the best views in Worcester. Each back porch held a clothes reel where the laundry could hang to dry in the beneficial sunshine. . . .

—Margaret Erskine

Send on your orders. Worcester will oil them, grind them, wrench them, shape them, drill them and envelope them.

—Worcester Board of Trade

When I was a boy in Worcester, Massachusetts, my family lived on top of a hill, at the thin edge of the city, with woods beyond. Much of the time I was alone, but I learned how not to be lonely, exploring the surrounding fields and the old Indian trails.

—*Stanley Kunitz*

The Loraxes and Grinches, the Cats in Hats and elephants on nests, began life not so far from Mulberry Street in Springfield, Massachusetts. The boy's sense of the absurdity of the adult rules came from his father, slated to be named president of a brewery on the very day Prohibition began. The fantastic menagerie grew out of [Theodor] Geisel's visits to the zoo when his father became, instead, Superintendent of Parks.

—*Ellen Goodman*

City of Homes
—late nineteenth-century nickname for Springfield

Every walk in the hills above the [Connecticut River] valley brought me into contact with the early settlers who scratched a subsistence from the shallow soil all but completely eroded from the rock ledge, many a farmer felled by the hernias that came from trying to drag the huge rocks scattered by the glaciers from fields they marked off by dry stone walls. Most secluded back roads led to small cemeteries where the hard granite gravestones told the history of families and towns.

—Jill Ker Conway

Northfield . . . belongs in an old lithograph. Northfield has houses
with hipped roofs and center chimneys, ones with pediments and
columned porticoes, ones with the pointy-topped windows of the
prototypical American haunted house. The late Georgian, the
Federalist, the Greek Revival, and the Gothic, all are represented
in the old houses of Northfield's streets.

—*Tracy Kidder*

There are a lot of people for whom Emily Dickinson is an icon. [In
Amherst] it's both a big deal and not a big deal. She's just one of us,
like a neighbor.

—*Jonathan Tucker*

For a town its size, Northampton has an unusually large number of lawyers, doctors, clergy, judges. An extraordinary number, about two hundred, work in the psychological trade—a few earn half their incomes analyzing fellow analysts.

—Tracy Kidder

Life flows on as evenly as ever up here [in Northampton]. Letters and scraps of news are very welcome. Sometimes it waxes so stupid that I swear a mighty oath that I will pack off the next day.

—Henry James

This must be the paradise of America.

—Jenny Lind, on Northampton

Northampton is the kind of place where a professor, potter, unemployed musician, former mental patient, a woman with a handsome alimony, can all be found on Sunday mornings sitting near one another at sidewalk tables outside the coffee shops.

—*Tracy Kidder*

My town [Great Barrington] was shut in by its mountains and provincialism; but it was a beautiful place, a little New England town nestled shyly in its valley with something of Dutch cleanliness and English reticence.

—*W. E. B. DuBois*

It is to the glory of Great Barrington that it had twenty-five heroes
who were willing to risk the destruction of their properties by sub-
scribing to the crazy scheme that [William] Stanley claimed would
give them light in their stores and offices. From the one-time rubber
factory two number eight wires were strung through insulators on
trees to the twenty-five guinea-pig hutches. . . . Darkness fell. Stanley
himself closed the switch. There was no sound. Suddenly and simul-
taneously twenty-five sets of windows along Main Street were seen
to be alight. In prospect all the future nights of the world were alight.
                                                    —*Chard Powers Smith*

It is probable that there has been more horse-racing in these two
towns [Great Barrington and Stockbridge] than in all the state of
Massachusetts besides. . . . The soil is excellent, yet we saw very
few marks of thrift or prosperity. The houses are in many instances
decayed; the Episcopal Church barely decent; the Congregational
ruinous. . . . Religion has had here, generally, a doubtful existence.
                                                    —*Timothy Dwight IV*

In Lenox you are estimated, in Stockbridge you are esteemed.

—*Stockbridge folklore*

Lenox has had its usual tonic effect on me, & I feel like a new edition, revised & corrected . . . in the very best type.

—*Edith Wharton*

It is very singular how much more we are in the center of society in Lenox than we were in Salem, and all literary persons seem settling around us. But when they get established here I dare say we shall take flight.

—*Mrs. Nathaniel (Sophia) Hawthorne*

[Stockbridge is] the best of America, the best of New England.

—Norman Rockwell

Naturally, the arrival of someone like Duke Wayne or Frank Sinatra caused a flurry of excitement in Stockbridge. Having Norman Rockwell and his guests around was more fun than a three-ring circus and great for the town's tourist industry. If it wasn't a movie star showing up for a portrait sitting, it might be someone like the fried-chicken tycoon Colonel Sanders, a big-wheel politico, or just some run-of-the-mill Texas oil multimillionaire or Wall Street mogul.

—Donald Walton

[Stockbridge is] a great little town. We have a democracy that works and a police force that's honest.

—Peter A. A. Berle

You cannot think how often Stockbridge and its landscape come into my mind. None of the cities could attach me, not even Boston, but I could get fond of Stockbridge. . . .

—*Matthew Arnold*

I spend six months of the year . . . in heaven.

—*Daniel Chester French, on his Stockbridge studio*

On circus day in Pittsfield . . . the hill dwellers descend into town to congregate on street corners and wait for the free parade. They are all there—from squalling infants in arms and small boys uncomfortable in tight shoes to housewives in homemade garments. . . . Many a group has its bearded grandfather who needs only a scythe to complete the illusion that he is Father Time.

—WPA Guide to The Berkshire Hills, 1939

Pittsfield is no longer the quiet, dullish, somewhat dingy village that some of us remember it, standing with Yankee reserve in the midst of fine scenery, where it seemed a little out of place. It has become of late years a bustling, ambitious . . . town . . . with fine public buildings, parks and fountains and an abundance of "carriage people."

—*Edward Boltwood*

Pittsfield is conceded to be the most healthy place in North America, there having been but a single case of genuine Asiatic cholera there for the last five years! The people of Pittsfield are exceedingly modest, and of great hospitality, but patrons of temperance; their gas is excellent, and their wine not wanting in age. . . .

—*Horace Taylor*

Seven of the happiest summers of my life were passed in Berkshire with the Housatonic running through my meadows and Greylock looking into my study windows.

—*Oliver Wendell Holmes*

Palaces that housed flashy wives of captains of industry; women who powdered their hair with gold dust, and were buxom counters for jewels: whose parties were prepared . . . by imported chefs and served by flunkies in knee breeches. The livery of admittance for their guests was a flamboyant appearance that advertised a rising bank account. No manners were required in these houses; no intellect. . . . The new society moved rapidly from New York to Newport [to the Berkshires and back again] so a changing environment would give them the illusion of thinking.

—*Nathalie Sedgwick Colby*

By the standards of the Ten Commandments, the "cottagers" were not any better or any worse than the general run of humanity. You get the impression that there were rather fewer scandals among the Berkshire rich than in most irresponsible groups, and in the second and third generations less degeneracy than is to be expected in the inheritors of great wealth.

—*Chard Powers Smith*

At least I'm the best dressed man here [in Lenox].

—*Edward Wharton, husband of Edith*

I'm on the road ten months a year, and I miss the Berkshires. . . . This is a beautiful part of the world, every part of it. We've been let down by the major industries. The only big industry that keeps growing is our cultural industry, so I'm anxious to see if we can all benefit from that.

—*Arlo Guthrie*

V

GET THERE AS FAST AS POSSIBLE

Driving in Massachusetts

The traffic rules and regulations in Massachusetts might be different from what you are used to in your home country.

—*Massachusetts Registry of Motor Vehicles*

Yes, everything you've heard about driving in Boston is true. If you're from some mild-mannered place like Nebraska, just turn around now.

—*Boston Online*

The first rule of the road in Boston couldn't be more clear: Get there as fast as possible. Rule two: Blow by as many people and cars as you can. Rule three: Ignore everything—yield signs, bumbling pedestrians, cracks in the earth's crust releasing molten lava—that gets in the way of rules one and two.

—*Peter DeMarco*

snail trail

—*Kevin O'Keefe nickname for Southeast Expressway*

You're from Boston if you know how to cross four lanes of traffic in five seconds.

—*Hub humor*

The results are in and after six weeks of online balloting and 16,561 votes, Massachusetts was named "The State with the Worst Drivers" in a SPEED Channel poll.

—*SPEED Channel News*

In truth, Boston drivers are keenly aware of the low esteem and absolute terror in which they are held by the rest of the country, and thus feel compelled to live up to that standard.

—*Grumbles Magazine*

You're from Boston if all the potholes just add excitement to your driving experiences.

—*Hub humor*

We say that cows laid out Boston. Well, there are worse surveyors.

—*Ralph Waldo Emerson*

In
Boston town
of old renown
the gentle cows
the pathways made
which grew to streets that keep the stranger quite dismayed.

—vintage postcard

A Bostonian, if he is thoroughly honest, would probably be willing
to say that it is not always easy for him to give another directions for
finding his way, or even to find his own way, through the maze of
streets that have been said to follow the windings of old cow paths.

—John T. Faris

The theory in Boston is that if you don't know where you're going, you have no business on the road. To hammer this point home, the city makes a point of putting up traffic signs that, if followed, will inevitably lead you to . . . the fastest possible route to New Hampshire, just to get you out of everyone else's hair.

—Grumbles Magazine

A Bay Stater would rather drive in bumper-to-bumper traffic for four hours to get to Boston than be caught dead on the Orange Line of the "T."

—Bay State humor

You're from Massachusetts if you can navigate a rotary without
a problem.

—*Bay State humor*

In truth, it's not that Boston drivers are that much worse than some
of their peers elsewhere. The difficulty of the course (which is to say,
the Boston streets) helps make them seem more frightening than
they actually are.

—*Grumbles Magazine*

Crush up a sheet of letter-paper in your hand, throw it down, and
there is a map of old Boston.

—*Walt Whitman*

I've wandered up,
I've wandered down,
The winding streets of
Boston Town –
But, with all the paths so
Neatly charted,
I've always ended where
I started!

—*vintage postcard*

The Bostonian . . . has reduced a pedestrian who crosses the streets
in disregard of traffic signals to the compact "jaywalker."

—Harper's Magazine

Yeah, the pedestrian is at fault. But if you run over the pedestrian, the judge is going to say shame on you. And that person's family is going to be living in your house.

—Brookline Police Sergeant Larry Fitzgerald on state jaywalking law

You're from Massachusetts if you've pulled out of a side street and used your car to block oncoming traffic so you can make a left.

—Bay State humor

Warning: Boston Pedestrian

—T-shirt

You're in Boston if cars are double parked on both sides of the street.

—Hub humor

Real Massachusetts female drivers can put on pantyhose, apply eye makeup and balance the checkbook at seventy-five miles per hour during a snowstorm in bumper-to-bumper traffic.

—WorcesterMass.com

A Boston car qualifies as vintage when resident parking stickers cover the back window.

—City of Boston parking enforcement officer

You're from Massachusetts if it's not actually tailgating unless your bumper is touching the car in front of you.

—Bay State humor

Tailgating is a Boston sport. I think most people do it subconsciously.

—former hearings officer for Registry of Motor Vehicles

bumper thumper

—Kevin O'Keefe term for touch-and-go auto collisions

You're from Massachusetts if you believe using a turn signal gives away your plan to the enemy.

—*Bay State humor*

Just because you're in the left lane and have no room to speed up or move over doesn't mean that a Massachusetts driver flashing his high beams behind you doesn't think he can go faster in your spot.

—*WorcesterMass.com*

Like a lot of Boston drivers I don't think twice about making a U-turn. Whether I've missed my street, or I'm stuck in traffic with a clear escape route in sight, I just bang a U-ie and all is well again.

—*Peter DeMarco*

Turn right at the Dunkin' Donuts, go down to the third Dunkin' Donuts and bang a left.

—typical Massachusetts driving directions

You're from Massachusetts if a yellow light is a sign to speed up.

—Bay State humor

Interstate Route 95, like many another road in Massachusetts, is forever incomplete. The signs bravely contend that this Detour is merely Temporary, but the same Detour has existed since I was born and reared in these parts, and I cannot be convinced that Interstate Route 95 will ever be finished.

—Raymond Mungo

lane sprain
>   —*Kevin O'Keefe term for traffic backup caused by lane*
>   *under construction*

[Nantucket] is proud that there are no traffic lights anywhere. . . .
There are at least four complicated intersections everyone knows
should have traffic lights, both for safety and to speed things up.
Everyone also knows it won't happen in the foreseeable future.
>   —*Frank Conroy*

Aggressive driving isn't an actual rule, but it does describe, with
embarrassing accuracy, how Bostonians often act behind the wheel.
>   —*Peter DeMarco*

Gawkablocka

*—Kevin O'Keefe term for traffic jam
caused by viewing roadside accident*

Never get in the way of an older car that needs extensive bodywork. Massachusetts is a no-fault insurance state and the other driver has nothing to lose.

—WorcesterMass.com

YOU ARE ENTERING GOD'S COUNTRY
DON'T DRIVE THROUGH LIKE HELL

—Berkshires road sign

VI

BREAD AND ROSES!

Massachusetts History

Georgia has sweet peaches, Florida has juicy oranges, Kansas has golden wheat. In Massachusetts, the bumper crop is history.

—Christopher Kenneally

Come Over and Help Us

—First Seal of Massachusetts Bay Colony

Of all the unlikely American success stories of the epoch, none is more improbable than that of the Pilgrims. They set sail to pursue their religion and live on fishing in a new world. The fact that they arrived at the onset of winter is the first hint of how little they knew about survival.

—Mark Kurlansky

They [the Pilgrim Fathers] fell upon an ungenial climate, where there were nine months of winter and three months of cold weather, and that called out the best energies of the men, and of the women too, to get a mere subsistence out of the soil, with such a climate. In their efforts to do that they cultivated industry and frugality at the same time—which is the real foundation of the greatness of the Pilgrims.

—*Ulysses S. Grant*

If April showers bring May flowers, what do Mayflowers bring? Pilgrims and furniture.

—*Pilgrim joke*

The Pilgrims: a simple people, inspired by an ardent faith in God, a dauntless courage in danger, a boundless resourcefulness in the face of difficulties, an impregnable fortitude in adversity: thus they have in some measure become the spiritual ancestors of all Americans.

—Samuel Eliot Morison

[A]s one small candle may light a thousand, so the light here kindled hath shone unto many.

—Governor William Bradford

The Pilgrims came to Plymouth in 1620. The plays of Shakespeare were not published until three years later. Had they been published earlier, our forefathers, or the most poetical among them, might have stayed at home to read them.

—Ralph Waldo Emerson

next to of course god america I
love you land of the pilgrims' and so forth

—*e.e. cummings*

In this the Pilgrims made their greatest contribution: they demonstrated that a colony could be self-supporting and encouraged others
to attempt the experiment.

—WPA Guide to Massachusetts

PILGRIM DADS LAND ON MASS. COAST TOWN
INTREPID BAND OF BRITONS, SEEKING FAITH'S PURE SHRINE,
REACH ROCK-BOUND COAST, SINGING AMID STORM

PROVINCETOWN, MASS., Dec. 21—Poking her nose through the fog, the ship *Mayflower*, of Southampton, Jones, Master, limped into port tonight.

On board were men with hoary hair and women with fearless eyes, 109 in all.

Asked why they made the journey, they alleged that religious freedom was the goal they sought here.

The *Mayflower* carried a cargo of antique furniture.

Among those on board were William Bradford, M. Standish, Jon. Alden, Peregrine White, John Carver and others.

Steps are being taken to organize a society of Mayflower Descendants.

—Franklin Pierce Adams

What kind of cars would pilgrims drive today? Plymouth.

—Pilgrim joke

The Pilgrims were a simple and ignorant race. They never had seen any good rocks before, or at least any that were not watched, and so they were excusable for hopping ashore in frantic delight and clapping an iron fence around this one.

—Mark Twain

This Rock has become an object of veneration in the United States. I have seen bits of it carefully preserved in several towns in the Union. Does this sufficiently show that all human power and greatness is in the soul of man? Here is a stone which the feet of a few outcasts pressed for an instant; and the stone becomes famous; it is treasured by a great nation; its very dust is shared as a relic.

—Alexis de Tocqueville

We have come to this Rock, to record here our homage for our Pilgrim Fathers; our sympathy in their sufferings; our gratitude for their labours; our admiration of their virtues; our veneration for their piety; and our attachment to those principles of civil and religious liberty, which they encountered the dangers of the ocean, the storms of heaven, the violence of savages, disease, exile, and famine, to enjoy and establish.

—*Daniel Webster*

Plymouth succeeded because its inhabitants did not come to the New World searching for glory, adventure, or hot man-on-Indian action. Rather, the Pilgrims had come to escape persecution, to create a society where they could worship as they pleased and one day, God willing, even do some persecuting of their own.

—The Daily Show with Jon Stewart Presents America (The Book) *by Jon Stewart, Ben Karlin, and David Javerbaum*

The Pilgrim Fathers incorporated a yearly Thanksgiving day among the moral influences they sent over to the New World. After our Independence the light crept slowly onward and westward . . . yet still it blessed and beautified the homes it reached.

—Sarah Josepha Hale

Our harvest being gotten in, our governor sente four men out fowling that so we might, after a more special manner, rejoyce together after we had gathered the fruit of our labours . . . many of the Indians coming amongst us. . . . And amongst the rest, their greatest King, Massasoit, with some ninety men, whom, for three days, we entertained and feasted. . . .

—from G. Mourt, A Relation, or Journall of the Beginnings and Proceedings of the English Plantation settled at Plimoth in New England, *1622*

Neither the English people nor the native people in 1621 knew they were having the first Thanksgiving. . . . We're not sure why Massasoit and the 90 men ended up coming to Plimoth. . . . And the idea that they sat down and lived happily ever after is, well, untrue.

—*Linda Coombs*

Thanksgiving Day is a reminder of the genocide of millions of their people, the theft of their lands, and the relentless assault on their culture.

—*United American Indians of New England*

The pious ones of Plymouth who, reaching the Rock, first fell upon their own knees and then upon the aborigines.

—*William M. Evarts*

They rose without hope and, therefore, they fought without mercy.
For them, as a nation, there was no tomorrow.

—*George Bancroft, on King Philip's War*

I am determined not to live till I have no country.

—*King Philip in 1675*

Before you come be careful to be strongly instructed what things are
fittest to bring with you for your more comfortable passage at sea, as
also for your husbandry occasions when you come to land. For when
you are once parted with England you shall meete neither markets
nor fayres to buy what you want.

—*Rev. Francis Higginson to prospective colonists in 1630*

What the Puritans gave the world was not thought, but action.

—Wendell Phillips

Oh, we are weary pilgrims; to this wilderness we bring
A church without a bishop, a state without a king.

—The Puritan's Mistake

Puritanism, believing itself quick with the seed of religious liberty,
laid, without knowing it, the egg of democracy.

—James Russell Lowell

Americans have always been a touch suspicious of leisure. Our Puritan patriarchs not only famously regarded idle hands as the devil's workshop, they believed the grindstone cleared the path to salvation.

—*Ellen Goodman*

The Puritans nobly fled from a land of despotism to a land of freedom, where they could not only enjoy their own religion, but could prevent everybody else from enjoyin' *his*.

—*London Punch Letters*

The Puritan's idea of Hell is a place where everybody has to mind his own business.

—*Wendell Phillips*

'Twas founded be th' Puritans to give thanks f'r bein' presarved fr'm th' Indyans, an' . . . we keep it to give thanks we are presarved fr'm th' Puritans.

—*Mr. Dooley*

Puritanism—The haunting fear that someone, somewhere, may be happy.

—*H. L. Mencken*

The Puritans may not have allowed theater or other entertainments in their midst, but for sheer spectacle they could always take a stroll through the Boston Common. Passersby might linger there at the stocks and pillory, the whipping post, and the gallows to enjoy thrilling demonstrations of the efficacy of leather straps, hot irons, and the noose.

—*Christopher Kenneally*

It was . . . the energy of the Puritans and the sagacity of their successors which made the name of Massachusetts famous wherever ships penetrate. It is no accident that the Indians of Vancouver Island still refer to all Americans as "Boston men." It is said that South Sea Island cannibals, before deciding to cook a shipwrecked mariner, used to enquire if he hailed from Salem. If so, he was rejected as too tough.

—*George Caspar Homans and Samuel Eliot Morison*

It was after the Revolution that Salem began her next great past . . . when her ships found ports known to no other vessels from America, and when, in crowded Eastern harbours, where the temple bells on anything but a Puritan faith chimed across the waters, it was Salem, not New York, nor Boston, nor Philadelphia, that was supposed to be the great city of the West.

—*Hildegarde Hawthorne*

From the 1780s until the Embargo of 1807 and the War of 1812,
when its prominence began to decline, Salem was synonymous with
the overseas luxury trade. Salem's merchants took great risks and
reaped great rewards in sending ships on long trading voyages "to
the farthest port of the rich East."

—*Salem National Historical Park brochure*

When I first arrived I found this province miserably harrassed with a
most Horrible witchcraft or Possession of Devills which had broke
in upon severall Townes, some score of poor people were taken with
preternaturall torments some scalded with brimstone some had pins
stuck in their flesh others hurried into the fire and water and some
dragged out of their houses and carried over the tops of trees and
hills for many Miles together. . . .

—*Governor William Phips in 1692*

A strong belief in the devil, factions among Salem Village fanatics and rivalry with nearby Salem Town, a recent small pox epidemic and the threat of attack by warring tribes created a fertile ground for fear and suspicion. Soon prisons were filled with more than 150 men and women from towns surrounding Salem. Their names had been "cried out" by tormented young girls as the cause of their pain.

—*Alison D'Amario*

It were better that 10 suspected witches should escape, than that one innocent person should be condemned.

—*Increase Mather in 1692*

The Salem Witch Trials of 1692 marked the birth of negative advertising in America. Pamphlets outlining allegations of witchcraft, citing specific details of its practice, gave accusations a gravitas that standing in the town square pointing at passersby and screaming hysterically "WIIIIIIIIIIIIIIIIIIIIIIIIIIITTTTTTTTTTTTTCCCCCCCCC-CHHHHHHHH!!!!!!!!" simply couldn't provide. But negative advertising proved short-lived in Salem society. Puritans soon grew ashamed of the evil practice and, as a sincere act of repentance, stoned the pamphleteer to death. Then, just to be safe, they drowned his family.

—The Daily Show with Jon Stewart Presents America (The Book) *by Jon Stewart, Ben Karlin, and David Javerbaum*

John Adams was not a Massachusetts man for nothing; he provided
for the rebirth of the New England fishing industry by informing the
British during the peace negotiations of 1783 that it was a case of
"fisheries or no peace."

—Waverley Root and Richard de Rochemont

By the eighteenth century, cod had lifted New England from a distant colony of starving settlers to an international commercial power.
Massachusetts had elevated cod from commodity to fetish. The
members of the "codfish aristocracy," those who traced their family
fortune to the seventeenth-century cod fisheries, had openly wor-
shiped the fish as the symbol of their wealth.

—Mark Kurlansky

[L]eave might be given to hang up the representation of the Codfish in the room where the House sit, as a memorial to the importance of the Cod-Fishery to the welfare of this Commonwealth.

—John Rowe, 1748

In the year 1690 some persons were on a high hill observing the whales spouting and sporting with each other, when one observed: there—pointing to the sea—is a green pasture where our children's grandchildren will go for bread.

—Obed Macy, on Nantucket

Death to the living,
Long life to the killers,
Success to sailors' wives
and greasy luck to whalers.

—Nantucket toast

Nantucket itself is a very striking and peculiar portion of the National interest. There is a population of eight or nine thousand persons living here in the sea, adding largely every year to the National wealth by the boldest and most persevering industry.

—Daniel Webster

So be cheery, my lad, let your hearts never fail,
While the bold harpooner is striking the whale!

—Nantucket whaling song

The imprinting of a young Nantucketer began at the earliest age. The first words a baby was taught included the language of the chase. . . . Bedtime stories told of killing whales and eluding cannibals in the Pacific. One mother approvingly recounted how her nine-year-old son attached a fork to the end of a ball of darning cotton and then proceeded to harpoon the family cat.

—*Nathaniel Philbrick*

[T]he girls of Nantucket at one time formed a secret society, and one of their pledges was never to marry a man until he had "struck his whale."

—*Whale Fishery of New England,*
published for the State Street Trust Company in 1915

Then I'll haste to wed a sailor, and send him off to sea,
For a life of independence, is the pleasant life for me.

—*Nantucket girl's song*

Nantucket is drenched with memories of the whaling days and the nineteenth century. It is sodden, to tell the truth.

—*Frank Conroy*

[M]any young men arrived in New Bedford daily. Coming by steamship, train, and stagecoach, it was not uncommon for a young man to leave the family farm one day and be off on a whaling voyage the next.

—*New Bedford Whaling National Historical Park brochure*

The only thing that was dispensed free to the old New Bedford whalemen was a Bible. A well-known owner of one of that city's whaling fleets once described the Bible as the best cheap investment a shipowner could make.

—WPA Guide to Massachusetts

one of the greatest assylums [sic] of the fugitives
—whaling merchant Charles W. Morgan,
speaking of New Bedford's role in the Underground Railroad

After a sojourn of a day or two in Philadelphia, [escaped slave] Samuel [Nixon] and his companions left for New Bedford. Canada was named to them as the safest place for all Refugees; but it was in vain to attempt to convince "Sam" that Canada or any other place on this Continent, was quite equal to New Bedford.

—William Still

She [Massachusetts] was the first in the War of Independence; first to break the chains of her slaves; first to make the black man equal before the law; first to admit colored children to her common schools. . . .

—*Frederick Douglass*

I waited until the captain went down below to dress for going ashore, and then I made a dash for liberty . . . when the ship tied up at the wharf at the foot of Union Street . . . I was over the edge and in the midst of an excited crowd. "A fugitive, a fugitive," was the cry as I sprung ashore. . . . Had never heard the word "fugitive" before and was pretty well scared out of my wits. But a slave had little to fear in a New Bedford crowd in slavery days . . . they stood aside and let me pass.

—*Joseph M. Smith,* 1830

While there is no single birthplace of industry, Lowell's planned textile mill city, in scale, technological innovation, and development of an urban working class, marked the beginning of the industrial transformation of America.

—*Lowell National Historical Park brochure*

. . . seems more the work of enchantment than the regular process of human energy.

—*Massachusetts governor Edward Everett,
on the growth of Lowell in the industrial revolution
of the early nineteenth century*

A city springing up like the enchanted palaces of the Arabian Tales, as it were in a single night—stretching far and wide its chaos of brick masonry.

—*John Greenleaf Whittier, on Lowell*

The textile factories built in brick, primly towered, solid, are ranged along the river and the canals, and all night the industries hum and shuttle.

—*Jack Kerouac, on Lowell*

In 1832, Lowell was little more than a factory village. Five "corporations" were started, and the cotton mills belonging to them were building. Help was in great demand and stories were told all over the country of the new factory place, and the high wages that were offered to all classes of workpeople; stories that reached the ears of mechanics' and farmers' sons and gave new life to lonely and dependent women in distant towns and farmhouses.

—*Harriet H. Robinson*

Lowell, with its steeple-crowned factories, resembles a Spanish town with its convents, but with this difference, that in Lowell you meet no rags nor Madonnas, and that the nuns in Lowell, instead of working sacred hearts, spin and weave cotton.

—*Michel Chevalier*

For twenty years or so, Lowell might have been looked upon as a rather select industrial school for young people. The girls there were just such girls as are knocking at the doors of young women's colleges today.

—*Lucy Larcom*

Niagara and Lowell are the two objects I will longest remember in my American journey—the one the glory of American scenery, the other of American industry.

—*nineteenth-century Scottish tourist*

Lowell decided that its identity was important. Important to its people and the Nation. There are hundreds of people who should be credited for discovering this America. Many workers . . . wanted the good and the bad of the past preserved, rather than flattened and denied.

—*Congressman Paul Tsongas*

Lowell is a sister-city to Lawrence and Haverhill, all three being
one-river towns born of the "industrial revolution" and very close
in spirit to those almost-charming images of factory towns in British
literature from Blake to the Beatles.

—*Raymond Mungo*

The slope behind our mills (the "Lawrence" Mills) was a green lawn;
and in front of some of them the overseers had gay flower-gardens;
we passed in to our work through a splendor of dahlias and hollyhocks.

—*Lucy Larcom*

Before Lawrence, I had known a good deal about labor, but I had not
felt about it. I had not got angry. In Lawrence I got angry. I wanted
to do something about it.

—*Mary Heaton Vorse, on 1912 "Bread and Roses" strike*

As we come marching, marching, we bring the greater days
The rising of the women is the rising of the race.
No more the drudge and idler—tend that toil while one reposes
But a sharing of life's glories: Bread and Roses! Bread and Roses!

—James Oppenheim

Back in the days of the famine many set out for Massachusetts from
my harbor, Derry. The song, Danny Boy—originally known as
Derry Air—is about a mother saying goodbye to her son, whom she
will never again see.

—John Hume, Nobel Peace laureate

We don't know for certain that the Massachusetts Legislature was the state's most exclusive speakeasy during Prohibition. True, contraband liquor was stored in the basement of the State House, but as for the accusation by the Massachusetts Anti-Saloon League that lawmakers celebrated the close of the 1927 session with a drunken party . . . well, the Legislature itself launched an investigation and found no proof of the charge.

—*Robert David Sullivan*

Many people think of Boston as the birthplace of democracy in our country. They may not realize it is also the birthplace of the democratization of investing. It was there . . . that three stock salesmen created the first mutual fund and opened up what was once an exclusive province of the affluent to just about everyone.

—*Anne Kates Smith*

There is no better place in the world to start a robotics enterprise than in Massachusetts.

—*Dr. Rodney Brooke*

Massachusetts is crawling with assets for biomimetic robot developers.

—*Joseph Ayers*

The day of the Puritan has passed; the Anglo-Saxon is a joke; a new and better America is here.

—*Massachusetts politician James Michael Curley*

VII

A SURPRISE
IN THE MIND

The Massachusetts Landscape

A man may stand there and put all of America behind him.

—Henry David Thoreau, on Cape Cod

[It is] only a headland of high hills of sand, overgrowne with shrubbie pines, brush and such trash, but an excellent harbour for all weathers. [Cape Cod] is made by the Maine sea on the one side and a great Bay on the other, in the form of a sickle.

—Captain John Smith

Solitary and elemental, unsullied and remote, visited and possessed by the outer sea, these sands might be the end or the beginning of a world.

—Henry Beston, on outer Cape Cod

The ocean, like an indecisive sculptor, putters around with Cape Cod, chipping off here and slapping on there, to suit its mood of the moment.

—Josef Berger

[Outer Cape Cod is] a rising horizontal Matterhorn, a flattened precipice projecting outward rather than upward, but an imposing eminence nonetheless, full of isolated grandeur.

—Robert Finch

Cape Cod is a one-story place. Everything sits against the horizon. Everything is in human scale.

—Joel Meyerowitz

It is roughly an hour from Boston to Cape Cod, but once I have crossed the Sagamore Bridge everything is different. It is then that summer begins.

—*Paul Theroux*

It was a place where people could lie on the ground and wear their old clothes.

—*Henry James, on Cape Cod*

Love in mid-afternoon in the remote crater of a sand dune—her solid soft human body after the hard rough grainy sand. —Limitations of nocturnal city love, love confined to beds and couches, I realized for the first time.

—*Edmund Wilson, on summering in Truro*

Cape Cod wears its heart on its sleeve; and wears it like a Christian on the very end of its sleeve in lieu of a fish. For where the arm of earth gathers protectingly about Cape Cod Bay, and its fingers enfold a harbor of a thousand ships, there is concentrated in a league of shore, village and dune the quintessence of the Cape's beauty and romance and dear, naïve humanity.

—Robert Haven Schauffler

the bared and bended arm of Massachusetts

—Henry David Thoreau, on Cape Cod

To understand this great outer beach, to appreciate its atmosphere, its "feel," one must have a sense of it as the scene of wreck and elemental drama.

—Henry Beston, on Cape Cod's "Great Beach"

For sheer power and visual spectacle, Nauset in a northeaster is better than a thousand Niagaras. Here we gather to peer over the edge of our land and watch our very foundations eroding away. At such times, the Cape seems no more than a low sandbar on which the ocean stumbles, momentarily, on its long, slow march toward the mainland.

—Robert Finch

Living on Cape Cod has given me a good notion of wind speed and air temperature. This complex landscape has taught me ways of measuring the world of risk.

—Paul Theroux

I always come back to the Cape and walk the beach when I have a tough decision to make. I can think and be alone.

—John F. Kennedy

[Provincetown] is not en route to anywhere else. One of its charms is the fact that those who go there have made some effort to do so.

—*Michael Cunningham*

The northern reach of Cape Cod . . . had only been formed by wind and sea over the last ten thousand years. . . . Perhaps this is why Provincetown is so beautiful. Conceived at night (for one would swear it was created in the course of one dark storm) its sand flats still glistened in the dawn with the moist primeval innocence of land exposing itself to the sun for the first time.

—*Norman Mailer*

The Platte River in Nebraska is said to be a mile wide and an inch deep. Hardly less remarkable are the dimensions of Provincetown. It is three miles long and averages little more than a stone's throw in width. It is a mere hand's breadth of civilization wedged between insatiate devils of sand dunes and the deep sea.

—Robert Haven Schauffler

To one accustomed to the fertile shores of Narragansett Bay or the valley of the Connecticut, the region between Sandwich and Orleans . . . is bad enough . . . beyond this is simply a wilderness of sand.

—Appleton's Illustrated Hand-Book
of American Summer Resorts

There is something fundamentally allegorical about [Cape Cod]
dune country: each feature—every bush, bog, ridge and buried tree
trunk—stands out from its background with a kind of concentrated
suggestiveness. The scale is small and uncluttered, an expressionist
landscape that seems created for parables and myths.

—Robert Finch

May and June in Provincetown tend to mist and fogs, and the town
is as greenly muted as a village in the Scottish highlands. The foghorn
blows all day as well as all night.

—Michael Cunningham

I love Truro. It's so raw and beautiful. Every night we're on the beach
and it's different, and every morning when you wake up it's different.

—Anne Bernays

Whether the traveler approaches [Martha's Vineyard] from Newport or from Wood's Hole, through Vineyard Sound, or comes past No Man's Land and the southern shore . . . he will have to own that there, at last, is "something different." . . . He may be one of the tiresome individuals who insist that it is impossible to take a vacation; but Martha's Vineyard will make him regret the years when he was foolishly insistent on working without a break.

—*John T. Faris*

Martha's Vineyard . . . had lived through the upsurge of mountains and their erosion, through the rise and fall of oceans, the life and death of great forests and swamps. Dinosaurs had passed over Martha's Vineyard, and their bones were compacted into the bedrock. Glaciers had come and gone, sucking the island to the north, pushing it like a ferry to the south again. Martha's Vineyard had fossil deposits one million centuries old.

—*Norman Mailer*

Nantucket! Take out your map and look at it. See what a real corner of the world it occupies; how it stands there, away off shore, more lonely than the Eddystone lighthouse. Look at it—a mere hillock, and elbow of sand; all beach, without a background.

—*Herman Melville*

Isolation from the world surrounds [Nantucket] with a mysterious haze.

—*Samuel Adams Drake*

Nantucket, which means "faraway land" in the language of the island's native inhabitants, the Wampanoag, was a mound of sand eroding into an inexorable ocean, and all its residents, even if they had never left the island, were all too aware of the inhumanity of the sea.

—*Nathaniel Philbrick*

Even in Revere, huddled near the city's towers and the airport's roar, the ocean lies at the end of every cross street.

—*Webster Bull*

I held a memory of the old Revere Beach in my mind's eye, the Dodgems, the Wild Mouse, the Cyclone, the smell of fried dough and pepper steak, the families who used to come down here by the tens of thousands on a warm Saturday morning like this and spread out their blankets and chairs. It was my little kingdom, this three-mile stretch of sand. . . .

—*Roland Merullo*

Nothing . . . presents a more striking contrast to the jumbled, noisy scenery of a great town [than] the grand and refreshing sight of [Revere Beach] with its long, simple, curve, and its open view of the ocean.

—*Charles Eliot*

With its back roads and shade trees, its sweeping landscapes and sudden ocean vistas, Boston's North Shore was built for a Sunday drive on a Tuesday morning or Friday evening.

—Webster Bull

Charles River . . . water is more clarifying to the brain than the Savannah or Alabama rivers; yet the men that drink it get up earlier, and some of the morning light lasts through the day.

—Ralph Waldo Emerson

I like to go to the mouth of the Charles and see the tide-waters spreading out sea-like, flashing and freshening the air. Then I walk with the sun at my back; and when he sets, return with all the glory full upon me.

—Henry Wadsworth Longfellow

At sunset on a hazy summer night the meadows along the Concord River offer a fortune in light and air and bird-life. The lazy green water drifts along, bound north for the Merrimack, in no hurry, falling less than a foot in a mile. It barely has the power to keep vegetation from its channel. It hasn't the energy to ripple its own surface.

—Ron McAdow

I could look out at the Holyoke Range from the [Smith College] campus and imagine the last collision of North America with Africa, which had thrust it up running east to west across the valley around Northampton. Those hills had once been the height of the Himalayas, their current gentle shape created as successive glaciers turned them into the low rounded hills that now rimmed the expanse of the Connecticut River and its floodplain.

—Jill Ker Conway

[Mount Holyoke] is a favorite place of resort. The view is beautiful and picturesque, and is pronounced by distinguished travelers to be the finest in America.

—*Burt's Illustrated Guide of the Connecticut Valley*

The view here far exceeds all I have ever had before.

—*Reverend Paul Coffin, on Mount Holyoke*

[Mount Holyoke] was important because the prospect afforded from the summit provided a combination of untouched wilderness, which in the nineteenth century was seen as a manifestation of God's power, and cultivation, which represented the progress of civilization— beautifully combined in one view.

—*Marianne Doezema*

I have been all over England, have traveled through the highlands of Scotland; I have passed up and down the Rhine. I have ascended Mt. Blanc and stood on Campagna in Rome; but have never seen anything so surprisingly lovely as this.

—Senator Charles Sumner, on Mount Holyoke

The western end of Massachusetts is the America I recognize more than any other.

—James Taylor

Almost every estate . . . strives to incorporate its particular view into the garden scheme, to make the enfolding Berkshire Hills forever a part of the domestic life pattern. That is what we think of our country. . . . If that isn't what you are looking for, and you are insensible to the subtler differences of landscape appeal and ways of living, I'm not sure we want you at all.

—Walter Prichard Eaton

Majesty is all around us here in Berkshire, sitting as in a grand Congress of Vienna of majestical hill-tops, and eternally challenging our homage.

—Herman Melville

I have never driven through such romantic scenery, where there was such a variety and boldness of mountain shapes as this . . . mountains diversified the view with sunshine and shadow, and glory and gloom.

—Nathaniel Hawthorne, on Hoosic Range

the lovely and the wild mingled in harmony on Nature's face
—William Cullen Bryant, on Monument Mountain

a headless sphinx wrapped in a rich Persian shawl
—*Nathaniel Hawthorne, on Monument Mountain*

I build many castles in the air, and in fancy many on the earth; and one of these is on the uplands of the Oxbow, looking eastward down the valley, across this silver Dian's bow of the Housatonic.
—*Henry Wadsworth Longfellow*

Every new aspect of the mountains, or view from a different position, creates a surprise in the mind.
—*Nathaniel Hawthorne, on Mount Greylock*

Greylock: our daily pleasure, our constant symbol, our ever renewed inspiration, for all who have fellowship with Nature.

—John Bascom

[T]he view from our deck in Adams of Mt. Greylock . . . lacks the scale of the Alps or Rockies to qualify as sublime. But for us the constant changes of seasons, days and hours are so special and fascinating that we call it "Our movie." First thing in the morning we step out to the deck to observe the conditions of the day and to see what the mountain is up to.

—Charles Giuliano

[Mount Greylock] is the highest land in the state. . . . Its southeastern front is extensively visible throughout Berkshire, and from high elevations in the states of New Hampshire, New York, Vermont and Connecticut at very great distances. . . . During a great part of the year, it is either embosomed or capped by clouds, and indicates to the surrounding inhabitants the changes of weather with not a little exactness.

—Timothy Dwight IV

The students and professors of Williams College have made [Mount Greylock] a place of pilgrimage. The first observatory tower was built by a company of men from college about 1830. William Cullen Bryant was among the students who haunted its forest-clad slopes; inspiration for many of his poems came to him while in these lofty surroundings.

—John T. Faris

On one side the eye follows for the space of an eagle's flight, the serpentine mountain chains, southward from the great purple dome of Taconic—the St. Peter's of these hills—northwards to the twin summits of Saddleback, which is the two-steepled natural cathedral of Berkshire; while low down to the west the Housatonic winds on in her watery labyrinth, through charming meadows basking in the reflected rays from the hill-sides.

—*Herman Melville*

VIII

YANKEE DOODLE IN A KETTLE

Massachusetts Food and Drink

The first New Englanders brought to this land a dismal culinary heritage. They found on arrival that they must apply the rules, if any, of English cooking to the odd provender on which the Indians managed to live. Some of the Pilgrim Fathers starved to death but none of them as far as I am aware perished of dyspepsia, wherein lies the substance of miracle.

—*Frederic F. Van de Water*

We could not now take time for further search or consideration [other than to land at Plymouth]; our victuals being much spent, especially our beere.

—Mayflower *passenger diary*

I'm going to go the whole rest of my life and never have to drink anything but good beer.

—Jim Koch, founder of Boston Beer Co.

You're from Massachusetts if you know what they sell at a "packie."

—Bay State humor

It was an Indian habit to stow away caches of long-lasting foods in various places where they might one day be needed; it was the Pilgrims' good luck to stumble on one of these caches, which kept them alive (some of them) over their first terrible winter.

—Waverley Root and Richard de Rochemont

The abundance of Sea-Fish are almost beyond believing, and sure
I would scarce have beleeved it except I had scene it with mine
owne Eyes.

—*Francis Higginson, 1630*

the meanest of God's blessings

—*Pilgrim description of clams*

The luscious lobster with the crabfish raw,
The brinish oyster, mussel, periwig,
And tortoise sought for by the Indian squaw,
Which to the flats dance many a winter's jig,
To dive for cockles and to dig for clams.

—*William Wood*

If New England has been, from its inception, home to preternaturally determined human settlers, to those who equate hardship with virtue, its Puritan and Calvinist roots are apparent in its diet, which runs not only, of necessity, to that which must have the toughness boiled out of it before it can be served but which tends to eschew, by choice, any spices more flamboyant than salt and pepper.

—*Michael Cunningham*

The Northeastern Indians made considerable use of fish, but the Pilgrims were slow to follow their example; they did not care much for fish, except eels.

—*Waverley Root and Richard de Rochemont*

Easy to prepare, thrifty to serve, and delicious to eat, fish sticks, it can be truthfully said, have greatly increased the demand for fish, while revolutionizing the fishing industry.

—1950s ad for Gorton's fish sticks

For three centuries, New England families gave thanks to their Calvinist God for cold baked beans and stale brown bread, while lobsters abounded in the waters of Massachusetts Bay and succulent gamebirds orbited slowly overhead.

—Douglas R. McManis

Where lies the body of that mute American who first married the pork to the bean? And name if you can the early citizen of Boston who suspected that between Cod-Fish and Brown Bread raged a mysterious, almost illicit Amour.

—Frank Crowninshield

[I]n 1993 the legislature finally determined that the *Navy* had been the original bean in the famous and venerable Boston Baked Bean recipe.

—Massachusetts Secretary of State

Massachusetts
Wicked Good Beans

—T-shirt

Baked beans are a very simple dish, yet few cook them well.
—Lydia Maria Child, The Frugal American Housewife

In those early days, towns used to give each other nicknames, like schoolboys. Ours was called "Bean-town"; not because it was especially devoted to the cultivation of this leguminous edible, but probably because it adhered a long time to the Puritanic custom of saving Sunday-work by baking beans on Saturday evening, leaving them in the oven over night.

—Lucy Larcom

Cape cod turkey

—slang for baked codfish

In 1677, in the hope of charming Charles II into relaxing the crippling restrictions of the Acts of Trade and Navigation, Massachusetts sent him a handsome food package—ten barrels of cranberries, two barrels of samp (cornmeal mush) and three thousand codfish. This was an eminently representative sampling of the colony's resources, but its donors may have been a trifle out of touch with the tastes of the Merry Monarch.

—*Waverley Root and Richard de Rochemont*

Bean porridge hot;
Bean porridge cold;
Bean porridge in the pot,
Nine days old.

—*Massachusetts ditty*

[Baked beans] became closely associated with the city of Boston and with the Puritan women who baked beans on Saturday, served them that night for dinner, for Sunday breakfast with codfish cakes and Boston brown bread, and again for Sunday's lunch. No other cooking was allowed during the Sabbath, which ended Sunday evening.

—John Mariani

I was invited to dine with Captain Irvin upon salt cod fish, which here is a common Saturday's dinner, being elegantly dressed with a sauce of butter and eggs.

—Boston visitor, 1744

I had no idea that saltfish could be so delicious until I tasted it in Gloucester.

—Evelene Spencer

Boston mackerel

—slang for salted mackerel

Cape Codders used to cure [herring] in the sun, smoke them and salt
them in tubs of brine, string them through the gills to a stick and sell
them to each other, a dozen on a stick. . . . [S]ome folks, it was said
. . . ate so much herring, and became so thoroughly inured to the
many little bones it contains, that it was a day's work for them to get
in and out of their underwear.

—Josef Berger

A Mashpee smoked herring, especially one plump with roe, and
good bread and butter—what a breakfast!

—Thornton W. Burgess

I got scrod in Boston.

—*T-shirt*

America, great among nations, nevertheless has no sole. Boston calls flounder "lemon-sole," and a hotel calls almost anything "fillet of sole." Usually it is selling you flounder.

—*Josef Berger*

Fishiest of all fishy places was the Try Pots, which well deserved its name; for the pots there were always boiling chowders. Chowder for breakfast, and chowder for dinner, and chowder for supper, till you began to look for fish-bones coming through your clothes.

—*Herman Melville*

[B]reakfast [in a Boston hotel] would have been no breakfast unless the principal dish were a deformed beef-steak with a great flat bone in the centre, swimming in hot butter, and sprinkled with the very blackest of all possible pepper.

—Charles Dickens

Eating fish balls for Sunday morning breakfast is part of Boston's tradition, like reading the *Transcript* or taking visitors to see the glass flowers.

—Imogene Wolcott

Oatmeal is simply a Proper Bostonian custom, and as such it has taken its apparently permanent place alongside such other recognized customs as the morning lecture and the afternoon walk, the trustee meeting and the charity bazaar, the daily tea and the anniversary dinner, the formal call and Friday Symphony.

—*Cleveland Amory*

A good Boston fish chowder is hard to beat on Monday or Tuesday, and impossible to beat or even substitute for on Friday.

—*David McCord*

Such a dish [fish chowder], smoked hot, placed before you, after a long morning spent in exhilarating sport, will make you no longer envy the gods.

—*Daniel Webster*

But when that smoking chowder came in, the mystery was delight-
fully explained. Oh, sweet friends! hearken to me. It was made of
small juicy clams, scarcely bigger than hazel nuts, mixed with
pounded ship biscuit, and salted pork cut up into little flakes; the
whole enriched with butter, and plentifully seasoned with pepper
and salt. Our appetites being sharpened by the frosty voyage . . .
and the chowder being surpassingly good, we despatched it with
great expedition.

—Herman Melville

There is a terrible pink mixture (with tomatoes in it, and herbs)
called Manhattan Clam Chowder, that is only a vegetable soup, and
not to be confused with New England Clam Chowder, nor spoken of
in the same breath. Tomatoes and clams have no more affinity than
ice cream and horseradish. It is a sacrilege to wed bivalves with bay
leaves, and only a degraded cook would do such a thing.

—Eleanor Early

Cape Cod Clam Digga

—*T-shirt*

A New England clam chowder, made as it should be, is a dish to preach about, to chant praises and sing hymns and burn incense before. To fight for. The Battle of Bunker Hill was fought for— or on—clam chowder, part of it, at least; I am sure it was. It is as American as the Stars and Stripes, as patriotic as the national anthem. It is "Yankee Doodle" in a kettle.

—*Joseph C. Lincoln*

Boston clam chowder . . . is pure elixir from the sea. It bears no resem-
blance to the Manhattan transfer which involves a powerful tomato
base reflecting the presence of the stiff or wire-haired variety of
clam: a dish wholly unpalatable to anyone living within gunshot
of Dorchester Heights, the Hill, or the Fenway.

—David McCord

Nowadays, all too frequently [chowder] comes to the table in a
thimble. You measure it out with an eyedropper. Yet, in its day, a
chowder was the chief dish at a meal. Though it has fallen from
this proud estate, it is not, not, one of those fine, thin fugitive soups
that you delicately toy with in a genteel lady's tea-room. . . . And
P.S.—Please don't serve it in a cup.

—N. M. Halper

As to bread, there being little or no intercourse with the South, rye and Indian bread was our only supply, and that not always thoroughly baked. The minister alone was indulged in white bread, as brown gave him the heart-burn, and he could not preach upon it.

—*Josiah Quincy*

[H]ow this New England bread got its name. . . . The story most often cited is of a Gloucester, Massachusetts, fisherman's wife named Anna, who gave her husband nothing but cornmeal and molasses to eat every day. One night the fisherman got so angry he tossed the ingredients in with some yeast and flour and made a bread in the oven while muttering to himself, "Anna, damn her!"

—*John Mariani*

[Parker House rolls] are as much a tradition in the United States as any bread. They were created . . . by the Parker House in Boston, which was one of the great nineteenth-century hostelries. They have been copied by every cookbook author and every baker in the country. . . . Parker House rolls should be delicate, soft, and rather sweet, typical of American rolls in the nineteenth century, and they consume butter by the tons.

—*James Beard*

Established before you were born

—*Durgin-Park slogan*

At Durgin-Park's [sic], in the heart of the market district, the crockery is thick and durable as gravestones, and the tablecloths are red-checkered. Strangers sit side by side. White-frocked butchers in straw hats bump elbows with State Street brokers and Harvard professors. And almost everybody orders Indian pudding.

—*Eleanor Early*

Boston is a city rich with up-to-date, polite places to eat. Durgin-Park is not one of them. Its wide-open dining rooms, with brusque waitstaff and elbow-to-elbow communal tables, are neither modern nor polite. The food is old-fashioned, and *Nobody gets celebrity treatment; nobody is even treated very nicely!* Like it or lump it. We like it!

—*Michael Stern*

Go to . . . Young's in Boston, and bribe the head-waiter to point out to you any "real old families" that may be present and watch their operations. Alas! Even then you may be disappointed. There are men of old family and high degree who eat unpleasantly—champing the end of the fork perhaps, as if it were a curb bit.

—Hints on How to Acquire Good Table Manners

This is Boston, after all. Even the fancy haunts have high-definition plasma televisions tuned to sports during the dinner hour.

—*Meredith Goldstein*

When you hang out with a bunch of 300-pound linemen, you tend to find the places that are the greasiest and serve the most food.

—*Patriots quarterback Tom Brady,*
explaining his teammembers' penchant for fast food and lots of it

The first time I ever ate oysters was with Artis [Gilmore]. He had six dozen as an appetizer! He said "My record is nine dozen. Or maybe even a dozen dozen." The guy is seven-feet-two and weighs 240, but wow, six dozen oysters for an *appetizer?*

—*Larry Bird*

Eat oysters, love longer.

—*Wellfleet Oyster Festival*

A Wellfleet oyster, especially in the colder months, is supernal: firm and immaculately saline, a little mouthful of the Atlantic itself.

—*Michael Cunningham*

I never could find out any difference between a party at Boston and a party in London, saving that at the former place all assemblies are held at more rational hours; that the conversation may possibly be a little louder and more cheerful; that a guest is usually expected to ascend to the very top of the house to take his cloak off; that he is certain to see at every dinner an unusual amount of poultry on the table, and at every supper at least two mighty bowls of hot stewed oysters, in any one of which a half-grown Duke of Clarence might be smothered easily.

—*Charles Dickens*

Nathaniel Tracy, to entertain properly the admiral and officers of the French fleet [during the Revolution], had the swamps of Cambridge searched for green frogs, which were served whole in soup at a formal dinner. The first officer who struck one with his spoon fished it out, held it up, and exclaimed *"Mon Dieu! Une grenouille!"* The French roared with laughter.

—*Richard Osborn Cummings*

Overlooking a scenic marsh in the heart of the clam belt, where towns have seafaring names like Ipswich and Little Neck, Woodman's defines a whole style of informal Yankee gastronomy. They call it "eat in the rough" around here, which means you stand at a counter, yell your order through the commotion, then wait for your number to be called. The food is served on cardboard plates with plastic forks.

—Michael Stern

Massachusetts cranberries have a fine reputation in the national market and are associated with the southeastern part of that state, which also happens to include Plymouth and the origins of that great American meal-centered holiday, Thanksgiving. Not a bad promotional tool for a food!

—The Encyclopedia of New England

He sowed, but others reaped.
—*Gravestone of Ephraim Wales Bull, who bred the Concord grape*

The proliferation of the fruit [the apple] into the western territories came by the hand of an eccentric but gentle man named John Chapman, affectionately known as Johnny Appleseed . . . [born] in Leominster, Massachusetts, in 1774. . . . Beginning in Pennsylvania in 1800—barefoot, wearing a saucepan for a hat, and subsisting on a vegetarian diet of buttermilk and "beebread" (pollen)—Chapman planted apple trees and started nurseries over ten thousand square miles of American frontier.

—*John Mariani*

[Harvard president Edward Holyoke] was in the habit of laying in each year thirty or more barrels of cider as he had to provide much entertaining. Late in the winter he would draw off part of his stock and into each barrel he would pour a bottle of spirit and a month later some of this blend would be bottled for use on special occasions.

—*George Francis Dow*

New England was perhaps a bit confused about tea at first; in Salem there seems to have been some doubt as to whether it was a drink or a food: the leaves were cooked, salted, buttered and spread on bread, a habit which understandably did not last long.

—*Waverley Root and Richard de Rochemont*

[T]ea drinkers have no reason to expect anything in the U.S. Americans turned to coffee for political reasons nearly 250 years ago. Tea . . . was the drink of royalists and collaborationists.

—*Matthew Engel*

I must not forget to mention the delicious coffee made from the pure Mocha bean which ended the feast. An old Salem sea-captain had presented my father with a bag of the choicest variety, and it was only used on great occasions, enriched by cream so thick that it had to be taken from the cream pitcher with a ladle, and by the sparkling loaf sugar of those days, and served hot and fragrant, in my grandmother's delicate old India china mugs.

—*Caroline King*

You're from Boston if there are six Dunkin' Donuts within 20 minutes of your house.

—Hub joke

In the North End of Boston, Wednesday is Prince Spaghetti Day.

—advertising slogan

It's largely thanks to the Boston cream pie that I'm the biggest politician on Beacon Hill—and getting bigger all the time.

—Governor William Weld, on the official state dessert

Chocolate and Massachusetts share a long history. The first chocolate manufacturer in America, Baker's Chocolate Co., began processing chocolate in Dorchester in 1780.

—*Lise Stern*

You're from Massachusetts if you call chocolate sprinkles "jimmies."

—*Bay State humor*

Boston has been an ice-cream region since the early 19th century, but the last 40 years have taken ice-cream mania to new levels. . . . We may not wear $5000 watches, but we indulge in a high-end ice-cream cone after a modest meal, a super-premium bottle of beer with our burger, a superb silk scarf to accessorize our thrift-shop clothes.

—*Robert Nadeau*

In the East credit for one of that region's first hot fudge recipes has been claimed for Sarah Dow, who bought Bailey's ice cream parlor in Boston in 1900 and started making the confection soon afterwards.

—John Mariani

You're from Massachusetts if you've walked to Brigham's for an ice cream cone "to go" in the snow.

—Bay State humor

You're from Massachusetts if you know what a frappe is.

—Bay State humor

And in the 1930s, Ruth Wakefield of Whitman added bits of chipped up semisweet chocolate to cookie dough and invented what became known as Toll House cookies.

—*Lise Stern*

In 1896 Fannie Merritt Farmer published *The Boston Cooking-School Cook Book,* which for the first time applied scientific terms and precise measurements to recipes.

—*John Mariani*

[I] careened around the stove and WGBH-TV lurched into educational television's first cooking program.

—*Julia Child, on* The French Chef

These pilots would not have worked in Bayonne, New Jersey. It had to have happened in Boston. Julia [Child] was a child of academe, well connected to Harvard people.

—*Russell Morash*

[*The French Chef* was] helping to turn Boston, the home of the bean and the cod, into the home of the *Brie* and *Coq* as well.

—Newsweek

After more than a century of symbolizing the Brahmins of Boston, and after 75 years of banning women in the downstairs dining room, and after decades of . . . such colorful entrees as scrod, cauliflower, and Indian pudding, Locke-Ober reopens under the ownership of someone who is: a) Irish, b) a woman, and c) a chef with a reputation for creativity whose dishes—skate wing in elderberry wine, for example—could jump-start pacemakers in the Men's Cafe.

—*Jack Thomas*

IX

So Many Ways to Flunk

Education in Massachusetts

Other American colleges have campuses, but Harvard has always had and always will have her Yard of grass and trees and youth and old familiar ghosts.

—David McCord

Many of you are justifiably nervous about leaving the safe, comfortable world of Harvard Yard and hurling yourself headlong into the cold, harsh world of Harvard Grad School, a plum job at your father's firm, or a year abroad with a gold Amex card and then a plum job in your father's firm.

—Conan O'Brien

This colledge [sic] is the best thing New England has ever thought upon.

—Cotton Mather

Harvard
A Tradition of Men in Interesting Positions

—T-shirt

⌁

Harvard University, if I may say so, could vanish tomorrow (in fact
it *may*) with no appreciable loss to the physical or intellectual health
of the nation. Those who wished to study Catullus would continue
to do so; and those whose lives are considerably less earnest would
doubtless find some other occupation, perhaps more rewarding, than
hanging out in the Yard.

—Raymond Mungo

⌁

You can always tell a Harvard man, but you can't tell him much.

—James Barnes

⌁

Sitting serenely on the banks of the Charles, like an aged dean in his study, Harvard has always been a wise uncle to Massachusetts and the nation. . . . Harvard has ever known what was best for the people, and it will let matters go only so far before saying something or doing something.

—Arthur Bernon Tourtellot

[T]his year I'm told the team did well because one pitcher had a fine curve ball. I understand that a curve ball is thrown with a deliberate attempt to deceive. Surely that is not an ability we should want to foster at Harvard.

—Harvard president Charles William Eliot

Harvard professors do not often commit murder.
—Harvard president Jared Sparks,
referring to the 1849 arrest of Harvard professor
Dr. John Webster for the murder of Dr. George Parkman

I know of no title that I deem more honorable than that of Professor of the Harvard Law School.
—Felix Frankfurter

[Harvard men were] bred to swim a hundred yards and to shoot pool in the back room of Leavitt & Pierce's; to dine downstairs at Locke-Ober's . . . to heed the call of the cocktail hour in the Ritz; to write . . . as Robert Sherwood did, or like Robert Benchley, to be terribly funny; to join the Fly or Porcellian; to lie dead, like John Reed, in the Kremlin, or like others, to rule over a nation.
—George Frazier

I should sooner live in a society governed by the first two thousand names in the Boston telephone directory than in a society governed by the two thousand faculty members of Harvard University.

—*William F. Buckley*

This is a Harvard bar, huh? I thought there'd be like equations and shit on the wall.

—*Chuckie, in* Good Will Hunting

There were so many great music and political scenes going on in the late '60s in Cambridge. The ratio of guys to girls at Harvard was four to one, so all of those things were playing in my mind.

—*Bonnie Raitt*

I just remember getting really drunk [in Harvard Square] and spend-
ing a lot of time trying to pick up a waitress. She went to Harvard.
I was really impressed. . . . Because, if you're over at BU, or if you're
at any school in this area that isn't Harvard, you have an inferiority
complex which I developed to a full-on resentment.

—*Marc Maron*

a carbuncle of cabals and cliques

—*Wallace Stegner, on Harvard University*

For generation after generation, Adamses and Brookses and Boylstons and Gorhams had gone to Harvard College, and although none of them, as far as known, had ever done any good there, or thought himself the better for it, custom, social ties, convenience, and, above all, economy, kept each generation in the track. Any other education would have required a serious effort, but no one took Harvard College seriously. All went there because their friends went there, and the College was their ideal of social self-respect.

—*Henry Adams*

I was at, but not of Harvard.

—*W. E. B. DuBois*

Not that long ago, attending Harvard was a promising development for a postadolescent, but, as they say in the equities markets, no guarantee of future results. Now, apparently, if you go to Harvard, you've got it made. You've won the Pulitzer, copped the Nobel Prize. The resume, the contacts, the careerism, the confidence, the killer mentality—Harvard is money in the bank, and lots of it.

—John Sedgwick

[A]s graduates of Harvard, your biggest liability is your need to suc-ceed. Your need to always find yourself on the sweet side of the bell curve. Because success is a lot like a bright, white tuxedo. You feel terrific when you get it, but then you're desperately afraid of getting it dirty, of spoiling it in any way.

—Conan O'Brien

Harvard
A Wicked Good School

—*T-shirt*

We measure everything today by the standard of Harvard.
—*Johns Hopkins professor Basil L. Gildersleeve*

What the hell, that guy John Harvard never did anything for Cambridge except give the city six lousy books on Protestant theology.
—*Cambridge politician Alfred E. Vellucci*

Four years was enough of Harvard. I still had a lot to learn, but had been given the liberating notion that now I could teach myself.

—*John Updike*

When Harvard men say they have graduated from Radcliffe, then we've made it.

—*Jacqueline Kennedy Onassis*

As you leave these gates and reenter society . . . you're in for a lifetime of "And you went to Harvard?" Accidentally give the wrong amount of change in a transaction and it's, "And you went to Harvard?" Ask the guy at the hardware store how these jumper cables work and hear, "And you went to Harvard?" Forget just once that your underwear goes inside your pants and it's, "And you went to Harvard?"

—*Conan O'Brien*

It was a heavy handicap for an American politician to have gone to Harvard and have an upper-crust accent.

—Alistair Cooke

It's an open secret that you have Harvard University and MIT that tend to tilt to the left in terms of academic biases.

—spokesperson for Senator Rick Santorum

To this day the Proper Bostonian never ceases to wonder at the large number of young men who, apparently happily, attend colleges other than Harvard.

—Cleveland Amory

Better dead than crimson.

> —*MIT response to proposed merger with Harvard*

Though it may not appear so, this system really only educates those people who go out and grab their education by its throat. You can get a degree by wasting time correctly for a few years, but we refuse to call that an education.

> —*How to Get Around MIT*

An MIT education is like drinking from a fire hose.

> —*MIT saying*

Hacks provide sunglasses for every MIT student to wear when MIT becomes too bright.

—*MIT dean Samuel Jay Keyer*

Cosine, secant, tangent, sine
3.14159
Integral, radical, mu dv,
slipstick, slide rule, MIT!

—*MIT cheer*

One of my fondest robot memories is of a gorgeous 1971 hydraulic arm at Marvin Minsky's MIT AI Lab in Technology Square that reached back under computer control and ripped out its own shoulder. Since then Massachusetts robots have overcome their suicidal tendencies and developed caring personalities, military and industrial applications, online avatars, and are now even vacuuming rugs.

—*Bob Metcalfe*

Staying at MIT means changing MIT. And if you change MIT, you're going to change the nation.

—*Student Action Coordinating Committee*

The next stage of my intellectual pilgrimage to nonviolence came
during my doctoral studies at Boston University. Here I had the opportunity to talk to many exponents of nonviolence, both students
and visitors at the campus.

—*Martin Luther King, Jr.*

A schoolmate from B.U. passed me on the street one day, and asked
if I had picked up my report card. B.U. seemed a thousand years in
the past but I drove across the river out of curiosity and asked for my
grades. I didn't know there were so many ways to flunk: X's, F's, zeroes
and incompletes. That was the official end of my college career.

—*Joan Baez*

I headed straight to the *BU News* office and offered my skills as a
reporter and photographer. . . . There I met the strangest and most
wonderful cast of characters I'd encountered in all my 18 years.
Secular-humanist nerds on dope. Hyperventilating social activists.
Blue-collar scholarship geniuses and eccentric millionaires' children
in mutually gratifying solidarity.

—Clif Garboden

At BC, we want our students to make the right decisions even when
no one is looking.

—Robert L. Winston

You confront your own identity right away when you go to Berklee.
Some people never saw who they were until they got there.

—John Mayer

A lot of people like to knock music schools, but I really enjoyed my time at Berklee and got a whole lot out of it. That is one of the few environments where you can go knock on someone's door, whether they are a sax player, flute player, or heavy metal guitarist, and ask them if they'd like to jam.

—*Steve Vai*

I next set my sights on Emerson College, an esteemed Boston school that specialized in theatrical and communication arts. I figured that was as good a place as any to prepare to become a comedian. . . . Emerson's dean of admissions looked at my dismal high school record and burst out laughing. This wasn't necessarily a bad thing, since I told him I aspired to make people laugh for a living.

—*Jay Leno*

Emerson is a known commodity. It's known that a bunch of well-known people in Hollywood come from Emerson, so it rings a bell.

—Television producer Kevin Bright

Campus on the Common

—Emerson College nickname

We built a college in the heart of the city and changed the whole personality of the college. And now we're in everybody's face.

—Emerson board chairman Ted Cutler

Boston is a big college town. A lot of people think it's very hip, very liberal, very permissive. And it is! In a lot of ways—except one! I go to a school where in my dormitory, you can have girls in your room. You can have drugs in your room twenty-four hours a day if you want! There's only one thing you're not allowed to have: a hot plate!

—*Jay Leno's first professional joke*

Wellesley teaches us that we will be rewarded on the basis of our own merit, not that of a spouse. To honor Barbara Bush as a commencement speaker is to honor a woman who has gained recognition through the achievements of her husband, which contradicts what we have been taught over the last four years at Wellesley.

—*Wellesley class of 1990 petition*

I thought I was headed to a place that would turn out tomorrow's leaders, not their wives.
　　—Katherine Ann Watson on Wellesley in Mona Lisa Smile

From its origin as a diversion on May Day, hooprolling has become a Wellesley institution. . . . In late May, seniors line up on Tupelo Lane and vie for the honor of winning the race and being thrown into Lake Waban. Originally proclaimed the first woman in her class who will marry, later the first to become a CEO, the hooprolling winner is now said to be the first person in her class who will achieve success, however she defines it.
　　　　　　　　　　　　　　　　　　—Wellesley College website

When I arrived at [Mount Holyoke] several of the students told me how much they liked my play even though it was "a period piece." . . . When I asked them to explain what they meant by "period," they said, "Well, the women at your time were so confused about sex and graduate school. We're not confused. We know we're going to professional school and we know all about sex."

> —*Wendy Wasserstein, author of*
> Uncommon Women and Others

The stranger who looks at this institution [Mount Holyoke], its splendid edifice, unsurpassed by any college building in the land . . . could hardly believe that it had all resulted from the persevering efforts of one Female. . . . The object of its originator was to furnish the means of a thorough education to promising daughters of the poor, as well as of the rich; and this object has been entirely realized.

> —Boston Daily Mail

The domestic work would prove a sieve that would exclude from [Mount Holyoke] the refuse, the indolent, the fastidious, and the weakly, of whom you could never make much, and leave the finest of the wheat, the energetic, the benevolent, and those whose early training had been favorable to usefulness, from whom you might expect great things.

—Founder Mary Lyon

I love this Seminary & all the teachers are bound strongly to my heart by ties of affection.

—Emily Dickinson, on Mount Holyoke

I should like at least to testify to the obligation which our higher schools for women are under to Mary Lyon and the institution which she founded. Most of them owe their very existence to Mount Holyoke Seminary; all of them are unspeakably indebted to the work which it has accomplished . . . in giving so clear and forcible expression to the truth that intelligence is as valuable in a woman's mind as it is in a man's. . . .

—*Smith College president Laurens Clark Seelye*

I began to learn that no matter how much I might know theoretically about women's institutions from studying their history, nothing had prepared me for the jolt of energy that came from experiencing one. In my first weeks, I found a delegation of Amazons in my office explaining politely but firmly that the crew needed new, lighter racing shells. How else could they win the Head of the Charles?

—*Smith College president Jill Ker Conway*

When I came to [Smith] college I was an adolescent nut. Someone
like me should not have been accepted at a serious institution.

—Julia Child

Autumn, and the faces of young women, nervous and expectant,
could be seen looking out at Northampton through the back windows
of their parents' cars—here and there a Mercedes or limousine with
diplomatic plates, more often a station wagon. Families emerged
onto Elm Street, lugging pieces of households down the sidewalks
toward the Smith College dorms.

—Tracy Kidder

The Smith campus consisted of a hundred and fifty acres of brick and ivy and rolling green hills, dressed for the occasion with hardwood trees and thoughtfully placed benches. There was even a tree swing that overlooked Paradise Pond and the expansive soccer field that lay beyond. Merely being in this glorious environment soothed any personal problems one might be struggling with. I found it more effective than Ativan though not as soothing as Valium.

—*Augusten Burroughs*

I also loved the lively, noisy sense of ownership Smith women displayed about the campus. I liked to listen to the spontaneously raised voices of students chaffing one another, or barracking in the heated rivalry generated by intramural athletic contests. I'd spent many years on coeducational campuses without hearing women's voices raised in unselfconscious ownership of place and event. The noise level at Smith was the sound of women in charge.

—*Smith College president Jill Ker Conway*

Smith College
A Century of Women on Top

—centennial T-shirt

Few persons can have a higher appreciation of the importance of
[Amherst College] than myself. . . . I look upon it as a young lion,
born at the foot of Holyoke and Tom, crouching here in sheltered
seclusion, in the center of the Commonwealth, acquiring muscle and
brawn and power, and destined to make its voice heard throughout
the land.

—Amherst College president William Augustus Stearns

Just as Amherst is great because of its individuals, so individuals can
become great because of Amherst College.

—Amherst College president Calvin Hastings Plimpton

In the early days [Amherst College's] few faculty members, all ministers, enlarged the intellectual horizons of the community. Its students, taking their meals with Amherst families, became foster sons who, as they graduated and moved into ministerial and missionary posts around the country and globe, vividly extended the connections of those who lived in little Amherst.

—*Polly Longsworth*

At the University of Massachusetts [in the 1960s] it was a common experience for students to rush into a classroom, bring instruction to a halt and make wild speeches about the glory of socialism.

—*William M. Bulger*

A purple cow seems an apt symbol for a small-town rural college whose culture has been described as both intellectually venturesome and surprisingly unpretentious.

—*Williams College admissions literature*

Name recognition is important. However, a TV appearance by Williams College shouldn't be an enrollment cause and effect. Our students are smarter than that.

—*Jo Proctor*

It were as well to be educated in the shadow of a mountain as in more classic shade. Some will remember, no doubt, not only that they went to college, but that they went to the mountain.

—*Henry David Thoreau,*
on Williams College and Mount Greylock

X

I RAN
BOSTON

Massachusetts Sports

I ran Boston.

—*Boston Marathon bragging rights*

It is a course that may be triumphed over but never defeated. To challenge the Boston course, you must be at your peak. Accept your limitations and, with thought and care, you will have a creditable race. But go for broke and prepare to be broken.

—*George A. Sheehan*

The first time I ran the Boston Marathon I turned to a man running next to me and said, "So, where is this Heartbreak Hill?" and he said, "We just passed it."

—*Joan Benoit Samuelson*

Never again. I doubt if I shall ever again run in a marathon race.
—*John J. McDermott, winner of the first Boston marathon, 1897*

When you win Boston, it's almost like winning an Olympic medal, maybe even better.

—Bill Rodgers

Still, Boston is Everyman's—and Everywoman's race, the runner's Woodstock. They fly in from Honolulu or take the Greyhound from Wauwatosa, Wisconsin. Or drive a battered van from Thibodaux, Louisiana.

—John Powers

I didn't want to run Boston to prove anything. I just fell in love with the marathon.

—*Roberta Gibb, first woman to run Boston Marathon*

To be sitting on the starting line is a triumph in itself.

—*Jim Knaub, five-time Boston Marathon winner,*
wheelchair division

I had as many doubts as anyone else. Standing on the starting line, we're all cowards.

—*Alberto Salazar*

Boston is the pinnacle. It's the event that showcases our abilities at their highest. Everything else trickles down from there.

— *Bob Hall, first Boston Marathon wheelchair athlete*

But you've got the best crowds of any marathon in the world at this particular point, going up Heartbreak into Brookline and Boston. That's one of the things that makes Boston unique: They know the race pretty good.

— *Bill Rodgers*

I just love Boston and its marathon, and it felt so good to set a world record there. Records are supposed to be unattainable in those hills, but I had mine. It was 2:22:43.

— *Joan Benoit Samuelson, on her 1983 win*

Some of my proudest moments as governor were presenting the laurel wreaths to the winners of the Boston Marathon.

—*Michael Dukakis*

It's spring and the saps are running.

—*early joke about the Boston Marathon*

I will never forget rounding the corner and turning onto Boylston Street for the final yards of the race. It's a striking sight. There are thousands of people there, spilling over onto the streets and sidewalks and up on the plaza near the finish line at the Prudential Center. It's all downhill, funneling toward the finish. It still ranks as one of the most thrilling moments of my life.

—*Bill Rodgers, on his 1975 win*

As a rower, Head of the Charles is just the holy grail. There's an excitement you won't find in any other race.

—*Jim Dietz*

As hard as it may be for their partisans to believe today, there was indeed a time when the Boston Red Sox did not exist. This flaw in the national culture was corrected in 1901.

—*Donald Honig*

The Red Sox are a religion. Every year we reenact the agony and temptation in the Garden. Baseball child's play? Well, up here in Boston, it's a passion play.

—*George Higgins*

A fatalistic gloom hangs over Boston. It is August and the Red Sox are in first place.

—Boston Globe, *1986*

I always tell my teammates that we have the best fans all the way around. It doesn't matter what is going on in the game. It doesn't matter if we're winning or losing. They enjoy whenever we do good on the field.

—*David "Big Papi" Ortiz*

I've Gotta Wicked Case of Papi Love.

—*T-shirt*

I played before the greatest fans in baseball, the Boston fans, and I know what you're going to say about *that*: Old Teddy Ballgame loved those fans all right. He spat at them and made terrible gestures and threw a bat that conked a nice old lady on the head one day, and he never tipped his hat to their cheers. And you would be right. But there came a time when I knew, I *knew*, they were for me, and how much it meant to me.

—*Ted Williams*

It came simply, after an agonizing wait like Odysseus limping home across a bed of coals.

—*Peter Gammons, on Carl Yastremski's 300th home run*

The star of the Red Sox is the Red Sox, which provides a more durable sort of devotion. They are what we have here the way Dallas has, well, football.

—*Charles Pierce*

We're just a bunch of idiots. We're going to throw the ball, hit the ball, catch the ball. We want to keep the thinking process out of it.
                        —*Johnny Damon, on* 2004 *Red Sox team*

Fenway Park, in Boston, is a lyric little bandbox of a park. Everything is painted green and seems in curiously sharp focus, like the inside of an old-fashioned peeping-type Easter egg. It was built in 1912 and rebuilt in 1934, and offers, as do most Boston artifacts, a compromise between man's Euclidian determination and Nature's beguiling irregularities.
                                              —*John Updike*

The old park just keeps on keeping on, deepening its fund of "history" with every passing season. Red Sox history, Boston history, our history. Like us, it is smaller and weaker, but also finer and nobler, than any of the competition.

—*John Demos*

When I'm in Boston, I always feel like I'm home. I almost cry, I feel so good.

—*Luis Tiant*

New England's parlor, a region's nightclub, and the Olde Towne Team's hearth. To generations of Americans, going to Fenway Park has been like coming home.

—*Curt Smith*

What is it with Red Sox fans? It's not enough anymore just to go to the game, you've got to wear all the silly Sox threads. . . . Look at crowd photos from the '50s, and everyone's wearing fedoras, not camouflage ballcaps turned backward. . . . I'm not suggesting a return to business attire, but I am saying the grandstand's being overrun by Grandma Clowns, guys wearing unflattering Sox schmattes.

—*Mark Shanahan*

I take a live-and-let-live approach to style at the ballpark. I'd feel a little weird being a 56-year-old guy wearing a Varitek jersey, but that's just me.

—*Joseph Abboud*

the best place in the world to watch baseball

—*Roger Angell, on Fenway Park*

And I'd like to walk on that field just one time. Major league parks just give you a certain feeling. I'd like to grab a bat too. I can guarantee you I could hit one over the Green Monster.

—*Larry Bird, on Fenway Park*

It is impossible to overstate what the Wall means to Fenway. It has changed the way the Red Sox play baseball, sometimes saving them, but more often killing them.

—*Dan Shaughnessy*

[T]he atmosphere at Fenway for midsummer Yankee games is like no other. Longing blends uncomfortably with envy and doubt; spasms of hope flutter against a heavy despair that rides on every pitch or swing.

—*John Demos*

What makes Boston—little old Boston up here among the rocky fields and empty mills—think that it deserves championship teams all the time? . . . The founding Puritans left behind a lingering conviction, I fear, that earthly success reflects divine election, and that this city built upon a hill is anciently entitled to a prime share.

—John Updike

Curse of the Bambino

—Red Sox excuse for 86 years between
World Series championships

It's white hot. It's a rivalry on the field, it's a rivalry in the press, it's a rivalry in the front office, it's a rivalry among the fan base. It's as good and intense a rivalry as any you could have.

—Larry Lucchino, on Red Sox versus Yankees

Never in the 101-year history of league championships has a team lost the first three games of a postseason series and then gone on to win the series with four straight. This comeback will now be the by-word of hope for all teams on the brink of elimination. 'The Red Sox did it in 2004.' It happened. It can happen again.

—Boston Globe

Hell Freezes Over
—New York Daily News *headline, October 22, 2004, when Red Sox beat Yankees for American League title*

FINALLY!
Amazing Red Sox end 86 years of frustration with Series sweep.
—Boston Globe *Headline, October 28, 2004*

. . . and number 1: We got Babe Ruth's ghost a hooker and now everything's cool.

—Curt Schilling,
on top ten reasons 2004 Red Sox won World Series

Gradually it began to sink in that we'd shocked the world—or at least the world that follows baseball. We'd made history. We'd done something that will be remembered lovingly until the death of the last Red Sox fan who watched that last World Series game. Fifty years from now, people will talk about where they were that day and what they were doing. And they'll mention all their dead loved ones who never got to celebrate the way they did.

—Johnny Damon

Looks like Jesus. Acts like Judas. (Throws like Mary.)
—Boston T-shirt after Johnny Damon signed with New York Yankees

The great thing about the Cape [Cod Baseball] League is that you can get so close to the players. You are that much closer to them physically and emotionally. On a typical weeknight at a Cape League game you can get right up there and be a part of the game. But even more importantly, you're making an investment in the future of baseball.

—Steve Buckley

There's something special about going over the bridge and onto the Cape, especially in the summertime. It's like going into another world, a fantasy land of baseball. Each one of the little villages is so involved in the game of baseball.

—Nick Zibelli

There's just something short of wonderful about Cape Cod baseball, but then—if we are to believe Henry David Thoreau and/or Patti Page—there's something just short of wonderful about Cape Cod.

—Steve Wulf

The Cape League still remains true to the romantic ideal of the game of baseball—that it is simply a game, to be played with nine men on a side, four bases, three outs, and a village full of people cheering for both sides.

—Christopher Price

I love the Sox, and we love the Patriots and all our professional teams, but [basketball] was the game that was invented here, and our linkage to history is what makes it appropriate for this to be the state's official sport.

—Governor Mitt Romney

There are two spring rituals in Boston: Lent and the Celtics in
the playoffs.

—*Frank Deford*

Most professional basketball teams are loved by their hometown
fans. Only the Boston Celtics are beloved throughout the world.
The Celtics have followings in Italy, Spain, Belgium, France, the
Scandinavian countries and throughout South America. Celtics T-
shirts have shown up in photographs from the jungles of Nicaragua
to the mountainous regions of the Soviet Union. Other teams have
histories; Boston alone has mystique.

—*Bob Ryan*

[O]n one of my first visits to Boston . . . I realized what a tremendous following the Celtics had and I knew that if I did come to play for Boston I'd really be thrown into the fire. I knew I would be stepping into something *big*.

—*Larry Bird*

The Celtics aren't a team. They're a way of life.

—*Red Auerbach*

Of course when I was a kid, I *hated* Red [Auerbach] and I *hated* the Celtics and I *hated* that damn victory cigar. I wanted to run up, rip it out of his mouth, and stomp it into the parquet floor. . . . Now, of course, I see Red as one of the great sports icons of all time.

—*Chris Wallace*

Only when I reached the Celtics did I really come to appreciate the joy of winning as a team. To begin with, the Celtics were the definition of a genuine team.

—*Bill Russell*

You can't put yourself into the history book with the old Celtic greats until your team can hang a banner of its own. The Celtics are all about championships. Unless your team has a flag up there, you can't really say you've played on the same court as Bill Russell. . . . You don't know anything about Celtics pride if your team doesn't have a banner.

—*Larry Bird*

We won seven of our championships without having a single Celtic among the league's top scorers. . . . [T]he fun part of basketball isn't shooting, it's winning.

—*Red Auerbach*

[T]here was a mystique about the Boston Garden, a powerful invisible force that did some strange things to our opponents. . . . The famous "parquet floor" was another one of those factors my teammates and I knew how to exploit. [I]t had slowly gained an almost mythical status among fans and opposing teams. . . . The parquet floor was an invisible power that worked on the opposition; it gave them one more excuse to accept defeat.

—*Bill Russell*

[T]he Celtics have never been about stats. They have been about winning and about sacrifice and, in the final analysis, about honor. . . . When it comes to tradition in basketball, there are the Boston Celtics and there is everyone else.

—*Bob Ryan*

When you talk about Celtics tradition, it's more than just a matter of winning. We didn't just play the best. We also wanted to look the best, dress the best, act the best. It was a certain championship feeling.

—Red Auerbach

These are our glory days, and 40 years from today we'll be spinning the tall tales of a coach named Belichick, a quarterback named Brady, and a band of gridiron brothers who dominated the NFL and demonstrated the true meaning of the word "team."

—Dan Shaughnessy, on the New England Patriots

We're fortunate in that both teams operate in a place that has the kind of passion for sports that we have around here, that's second to none in Western civilization.

—Larry Lucchino, on the Red Sox and Patriots

The Patriots were not necessarily America's Team, as Dallas had so optimistically named itself in an earlier era, but they were an easy team for ordinary football fans to like in the new era of football.

—*David Halberstam*

And now the Patriots have . . . the 26-year-old guy who's already won a Super Bowl, who never loses his cool. . . . Oh, and he's also single, Damonesque handsome, humble, rich, and charming. He's secure enough in his manhood to admit to ESPN Magazine that he has his hair professionally highlighted and he carries a "European handbag," a.k.a. a purse.

—*Michael Smith, on quarterback Tom Brady*

[I]t's a team without an ego; all they want to do is win.

—*Kevin Spence, on the Patriots*

These players, a lot of other people didn't believe in them, but they believe in themselves. And that is all that matters.

—Bill Belichick, on the Patriots

[W]henever all the dynasty talk begins in earnest, it starts with the former sixth-round draft choice from Michigan, who has earned his rightful place among Boston legends Bill Russell, Bobby Orr, Larry Bird, and Ted Williams.

—Jackie MacMullan, on Tom Brady

None of this would be possible without the fans back in Boston. We'll be back [tomorrow] for the parade!

—Tom Brady, on winning the Patriots' second Super Bowl

So let those Big-Ten behemoths laugh at Harvard-Yale. We still like The Game. It tells us that it's time to lower the storm windows. It speaks to a certain purity of college sport. Sometimes, it even produces a gem of a football game.

—Don Shaughnessy

There are many good fans around the league, but I consider Boston's the best. They know the game and don't let us forget it.

—Bobby Orr

[T]he logo has come to symbolize both the hungry heart and the lunchpail ethic of a team whose style has characteristically been two-thirds ballet and one-third street fight.

—*Richard A. Johnson, on the Boston Bruins*

What I liked most about the Big, Bad Bruins, as people used to call us (actually we were the Big, Good Bruins), was that we always knew when to stop the joking and turn to the more serious matters of hockey.

—*Bobby Orr*

XI

CLASSIEST JUKEBOX IN THE WORLD

Massachusetts Fine and Performing Arts

The [Boston] Pops concerts are a good melting pot of music. I guess we're the classiest jukebox in the world.

—*Arthur Fiedler*

My first Fourth of July with the Boston Pops was pretty memorable; you don't know what it's like to perform in front of half a million people until, well, until you've done it!

—*Keith Lockhart*

You must go [to Symphony Hall] to see old Boston on parade.

—*Eleanor Early*

[T]he Esplanade becomes one of the most magical, romantic spots in America. The sun sets in the northwest and the moon rises over Beacon Hill. The music is played by a great orchestra under a great conductor. . . . And the music wafts and drifts on the air.

—David G. Mugar

Arthur [Fiedler] had a reputation around Boston as something of a rain god. The legend began one evening in 1949 during an Esplanade performance, when a storm wave threatened the concert. Turning and looking up toward the dark sky, Arthur lifted his baton, motioning the black clouds away. The sky suddenly brightened. At about ten o'clock, as the concert was concluding, there was a terrific clap of thunder.

—Harry Ellis Dickson

August 15, 1945 . . . we had over forty thousand people here at the Esplanade for a special Victory Program. Japan had surrendered the day before. I must have gotten a dozen letters afterward, telling me they met their future husbands or wives at that concert.

—*Arthur Fiedler*

Somehow I really relax [in Boston]. Sleep comes naturally. I've bought two suits, had a massage and gotten a haircut. And this phenomenal orchestra makes me terribly happy. What a response they give me.

—*Leonard Bernstein*

When I was a small child, a Symphony audience looked exactly as it does today. . . . I think that when this year's debs are another day's spinsters, they will save all their perfectly good clothes and they will wear them to Symphony on Fridays. They will arrive in the family's old car. . . . And they will smile gently at the men who did not marry them.

—Eleanor Early

After attending a Boston Celtics basketball game where the National Anthem was played before the game, Arthur [Fiedler] decided against playing it at the beginning of Esplanade Concerts; it would be too much like a sporting event.

—Harry Ellis Dickson

At Tanglewood sex was not a thing. You were too busy making music.

—Leonard Bernstein

My job is to make a situation where the musicians can have fun and pleasure in making music.

—Boston Symphony Orchestra conductor Seiji Ozawa

Yes, we do have fun, but we don't like to make it *too* obvious.

—Arthur Fiedler

The Boston Pops concerts aren't regarded seriously as a musical event. He is not a teacher of the masses. Arthur Fiedler and the Boston Pops are a slam-bang, cram operation for people who don't listen to music. Most of the stuff is what you get on Muzak.

—Michael Steinberg

To be a poet [in Boston] was not only to be good society, but almost to be good family.

—*William Dean Howells*

Shortly after we'd arrived at our new house . . . not far from Boston and Harvard Square, my father took us to see a new phenomenon, the "coffee houses," where you could order a cup of coffee or tea, no alcohol, and sit around in a stimulating intellectual atmosphere. . . . I wanted to move into Harvard Square and fall in love with every guitar player and singer I met.

—*Joan Baez*

The last thing I wanted was to be in a Boston band. If you were from Boston back then, you were either a folkie into blues or you were into more intellectual rock, which I thought was pretentious.

—*Steven Tyler*

Those of us who came out onto Massachusetts Avenue from the
Savoy Café to find our various ways home occasionally walked in
jazz time.

—*Nat Hentoff*

Back in Boston, I discovered that great starting ground for so many
comics: strip clubs! Since the early days of burlesque, these places always had a guy come out and tell jokes between every dancer's turn
onstage. I guess it was supposed to break the horrible monotony of
ogling bare flesh.

—*Jay Leno*

Whatever the reasons—huge college crowds, baked beans, Red Sox
and Patriot energy—Boston is to comics what Seattle is to a cup of Joe.

—*Laughlin Entertainer*

I was a tyrant on stage [at Club 47 in Cambridge]. If some innocent student wandered into the coffee house thinking it was like all the others, namely a place to relax and read, he was mistaken. I'd stop in the middle of a song and tell him that if he wanted to study he could use the library.

—*Joan Baez*

I'd quickly learned that comedy didn't exactly fit with most entertainment policies of the era. The coffee houses preferred their angry folk singers and poets who hated their parents. Which was fine. So I decided to bypass those places and seek out bars and taverns that happened to have stages.

—*Jay Leno*

If some band I really liked was playing at the Psychedelic Supermarket, this ex-garage rock joint on Commonwealth Avenue near Kenmore Square, I would go down for the day and visit the head shops. . . . It was strawberry incense, black light rooms, and underground comic books. . . . There was this whole new culture that was happening.

—*Tom Hamilton*

The history of Boston rock and roll begins with these immortal words: "Ding! Dong! Ding ding dong! Kading dong, ding dong ding!"

—*Brett Milano*

Boston Garden was like a holy place. . . . On July 18, 1972, the Rolling Stones played the Garden. It was like a papal visitation for us. . . . The next day their stage was still set up for the second night's show, and Steven [Tyler] and I walked out on it. . . . Steven said, "Wow. Wouldn't it be great to play here someday?" And I just thought, *Well, man, someday*. In three years, that was our stage.

—*Joe Perry*

I wrote "Make It" in a car driving from New Hampshire to Boston. There's that hill you come over and see the skyline of Boston, and I was sitting in the backseat thinking, *What would be the greatest thing to sing for an audience if we were opening up for the . . . Stones? What would the lyrics say?*

—*Steven Tyler*

Before Carly [Simon] opened the club most of the partying on [Martha's Vineyard] was restricted to small pubs or private parties. This was the start of a new nightlife scene. . . . We no longer had to drive miles to have a good night out. The only thing we worried about was staying sober enough to get home in one piece without stumbling into the ocean.

—*John Belushi*

Boston rock was born in the shadow of the city's Puritan heritage, and in some respects it's been kicking against that heritage ever since.

—*Brett Milano*

Boston [theater] audiences, being knowledgeable, are much more likely to react as New Yorkers will.

—*Elliot Norton*

Boston became nationally famous for banning things. In 1929, 60 books were banned, including some by Hemingway and Whitman. That same year, people who wanted to see Eugene O'Neill's "Strange Interlude" had to go to Quincy.

—Douglas Martin

It is expensive in Boston. It is better you should bomb somewhere else.

—John Corry, on theatrical tryouts

"Banned in Boston" could still beat a rave review, turning a real lemon into the showbiz equivalent of forbidden fruit.

—Diana West

I think Boston is being made ridiculous. A play [*Strange Interlude* by Eugene O'Neill] that has won the Pulitzer Prize, and that has been shown in the principal intelligent cities of the world, should be given a show here. The fuss over its showing in Boston is more like the action of a hick town than a metropolitan city.

—*Mayor John J. Fitzgerald*

We are thought of as unique, an American city which forbids or mutilates by censorship what is accepted as true or beautiful, or at least harmless, in the rest of the United States. The phrase "Banned in Boston" is considered funny now, but over the years it has raised tempers and stirred wrath among our own citizens and outlanders, too.

—*Elliot Norton*

[T]he prospect of being "Banned in Boston" caused playwrights to gnash their teeth, producers to bite their nails, and intellectuals to tear their hair. . . . Whitman, Hemingway, even "Snow White" were all banished for a time from the city.

—*Diana West*

That whole "Banned in Boston" business? That was a bad thing. We spent a couple of centuries trying to convince the rest of the country that sex didn't make us any more crazy than it made everyone else, that we didn't believe Libido was an old bistro on Hanover Street.

—*Charles P. Pierce*

To Hollywood types, Bostonians are rather like the Stone Age tribes that mad Englishmen in pith helmets used to come upon in strange places. . . . Boston accents by non-natives on the big screen are almost always ghastly. Movie scripts miss our song and cadence, our insular jokes and tribal self-flagellation.

—*Sam Allis*

[Matt] Damon and [Mark] Wahlberg were really stern with me to make me understand that the Boston accent had been butchered in cinema in the past and that I would be the laughingstock of their hometown if I didn't get this accent down.

—*Leonardo DiCaprio, on his role in* The Departed

[*The Departed*] was always going to be a character piece, a tone piece as well as a thriller. . . . I was thinking about the past, the people I'd lost, and what it was like for me as a kid in Boston, being angry and not knowing where to go or what to do. I was thinking about the mysteries of an Irish Catholic upbringing I hadn't solved yet.

—*William J. Monahan*

You just don't find a small town with the kind of artists that came to Provincetown and continue to come through here, as well as the writers, and actors, and playwrights. It's amazing; it truly is.

—*Christine McCarthy*

What is it sickens with disgust the Gloucester sailorman?
It's these everlastin' artists a'setting all around.
A 'paintin' everything we do from the top mast to the ground . . .
For they puts us in picters and they think it's just immense.
They call it "Picturesque," b'lieve, but it certain isn't sense.

—*Cape Ann ditty*

Were it not for portraits, art would be unknown in this place.

—*John Singleton Copley, on colonial Boston*

They dress the bacchantes
In bicycle panties

—*Boston ditty, on clothed statues in Public Library*

The aesthetic perfection of all things seemed to have a peculiar effect on the company [on the opening night of the Gardner Museum.] . . . It was a very extraordinary and wonderful moral influence. . . . Quite in the line of a Gospel miracle!

    —*William James, on the opening night of the Gardner Museum*

When Boston's ICA opened in 1936, Salvador Dali rode the train from New York to South Station costumed as a lobster, and he was the star of the ball, which was one of the glossiest social events in Boston's drab social history.

    —*David Bonetti*

XII

His Hat
Still Fit

About Massachusetts People

His hat still fit.
  —*North Cambridge neighbors, on Thomas P. "Tip" O'Neill*

A man must be a born fool who voluntarily engages in controversy with [John Quincy] Adams on a question of fact. I doubt whether he was ever mistaken in his life.

  —*Henry Clay*

[Abigail Adams] would have been a better President than her husband.
  —*Harry Truman*

[O]ver the years, heaven knows, this newspaper has had its policy differences with the senior senator. But it is also true that no single individual in political life today has done more for this state and its people than Ted Kennedy.

—Boston Herald

The Secret Service has announced it is doubling its protection for John Kerry. You can understand why—with two positions on every issue, he has twice as many people mad at him.

—*Jay Leno*

Jack Kennedy, of course, was a Democrat. But . . . I'd have to say that he was only nominally a Democrat. He was a Kennedy, which was more than a family affiliation. It quickly developed into an entire political party, with its own people, its own approach, and its own strategies.

—*Thomas P. "Tip" O'Neill*

The enviably attractive nephew who sings an Irish ballad for the company and then winsomely disappears before the table-clearing and dishwashing begin.

—Lyndon B. Johnson, on John F. Kennedy

Mayor of the Poor

—James Michael Curley nickname

Vote often and early for James Michael Curley.

—Boston street jingle

[John F.] Kennedy the politician exuded that musk odour which acts as an aphrodisiac to many women.

—Theodore H. White

So many politicians try to overwhelm you with their importance, their handshake, their wealth. [John F. Kennedy] was just a good guy.

—*Theodore Sorensen*

If Tom Brady were a politician he'd be John F. Kennedy—handsome, charming, and ever the winner. Making it to the top at a young age. The Camelot quarterback.

—*Dan Shaughnessy*

[Bill Belichick] dressed as simply as he could—his attire was as gray as he could make it, with the grayest of sweatshirts, and, as the television host David Letterman once said, he looked like a Sherpa guide on the sidelines. . . . There was no stylist to the Boston elite eager to take credit for his haircuts.

—*David Halberstam*

Red Auerbach is also a very fussy man, particularly about his clothes. Sometimes Red will show up in such sartorial splendor that he nearly blinds us.

—Bob Cousy

[Tom Brady is] the Eric Clapton of quarterbacks—if he works off the written music he'll never miss a note, but when you need him to improvise, he'll always amaze you.

—Sal Paolantonio

Of all the people I play against, the only one I truly *fear*—or worry about—is Larry Bird. Whenever we play Boston, it's always in the back of my mind that no matter what the game situation is Larry Bird can come back and beat us.

—Magic Johnson

At press conferences he sometimes seems a little goofy and is often way too grim. But he is a leader without the swagger, selfishness, and pomposity that so many men in business, politics, and sports embrace as an entitlement of their gender and position.

—*Joan Vennochi, on Bill Belichick*

Back in the days when men were men and women were damn glad of it, the man most men wanted to be was a boxer with swaggering virility named John L. Sullivan—simply stated, the strongest man in the world.

—*Bert Randolph Sugar, on the Boston Strong Boy*

[Massachusetts] had done many great things; she has given to our country many scholars, and statesmen, many poets and philosophers, many discoverers and inventors; but no son of hers has won for her a more enduring honor, or for himself a more enduring fame than William Lloyd Garrison. No one of her sons has stamped his convictions in lines so clear, deep and ineffaceable into the very life and future of the Republic.

—*Frederick Douglass*

Of the creative spirits that flourished in Concord, Massachusetts, during the middle of the nineteenth century, it might be said that Hawthorne loved men but felt estranged from them, Emerson loved ideas more than men, and Thoreau loved himself.

—*Leon Edel*

I could readily see in Emerson a gaping flaw. It was the insinuation that had he lived in those days when the world was made, he might have offered some valuable suggestions.

—Herman Melville

Emerson is one who lives instinctively on ambrosia—and leaves everything indigestible on his plate.

—Friedrich Nietzsche

[Thoreau's] senses seem double and give him access to secrets not read easily by other men, his observation is wonderful, his sagacity like the bee and beaver, the dog and the deer, the most gifted in this way of any man I have known.

—Louisa May Alcott

Whatever question there may be of [Thoreau's] talent, there can be none I think of his genius. It was a slim and crooked one, but it was eminently personal.

—*Henry James*

Henry James has a mind so fine that no idea could violate it.

—*T. S. Eliot*

Henry James was one of the nicest old ladies I ever met.

—*William Faulkner*

[Henry] James' cosmopolitanism is, after all, limited; to be really cosmopolitan, a man must be at home even in his own country.

—*Thomas Wentworth Higginson*

[George Santayana] stood on the flat road to heaven and buttered slides to hell for all the rest.

—*Oliver Wendell Holmes, Jr.*

Longfellow is to poetry what the barrel-organ is to music.

—*Van Wyck Brooks*

Dr. Seuss, the creation and the creator, was unlike most adults. He remembered. He retained a sense of the absurd, including the absurdity of the idea that growing up means losing your humor. So, while too many adults spend their time teaching children the seriousness of the situation, he managed to sneak under the heavy door of learning, asking, "Do you like green eggs and ham?"

—*Ellen Goodman*

She writes the strangest poems, and very remarkable ones. She is in many respects a genius.

—Mabel Loomis Todd, on Emily Dickinson

That's not writing—that's typing.

—Truman Capote, on Jack Kerouac

Kerouac opened a million coffee bars and sold a million pairs of Levis to both sexes. Woodstock rises from his pages.

—William Burroughs

Kerouac, you're blowing my mind living in Lowell. . . . Frost came from Lawrence, too, hey from my neighborhood in South Lawrence, but he *got out* man and he didn't come back. Robert Frost! And didn't Jack Kennedy make him poet laureate or something? Kerouac, see: Leonard *Bernstein* came from here, but *he* got out! Everybody from Lowell and Lawrence had half a break in the world *split.* You stay here, you're as good as dead baby.

—*Raymond Mungo*

I continually thank god for Arthur Fiedler, at whose hands I first heard live orchestral music.

—*Leonard Bernstein*

Call me Maestro.

—*Arthur Fiedler*

I have never known a conductor who enjoyed rehearsals more than Arthur [Fiedler] did. His approach to the orchestra was basically that of an antagonist—a bullfighter in the ring, with the orchestra as his adversary.

—Harry Ellis Dickson

Biggest Wuss in popular music

—Blender magazine, on James Taylor

How tough is James Taylor? He's tough enough to make a career out of being sensitive.

—Livingston Taylor

That he is indeed one of the very greatest masters of painting, is my opinion. And I may add that in this opinion Mr. [James Abbott McNeill] Whistler himself entirely concurs.

—*Oscar Wilde*

Isabella Stewart Gardner is the one and only real potentate I have ever known. She lives at a rate of intensity and with a reality that makes other lives seem pale, thin and shadowy.

—*Bernard Berenson*

[T]he great era of art collecting and the taste for the old masters in America were born with Isabella Stewart Gardner.

—*Aaline Saarinen*

This country was a waste-land of Philistinism in terms of food until ("food affirming") Julia Child came on the scene. . . . [S]he is one of those figures in history who totally transformed American culture.

—*Camille Paglia*

A pioneer of pleasure in a puritan country.

—*Noel Riley Fitch, on Julia Child*

A Harvard friend and neighbor who has filled the air with common sense and uncommon scents. Long may her souffles rise. *Bon appetit.*

—*citation awarding honorary doctorate to Julia Child*

Julia breathes hard and loves food. She is human. She is plump. She can be messy, a bit clumsy . . . she can drop a duck on her foot without coming apart at the seams.

—*Gael Greene*

Julia Child is the Chuck Berry of *haute cuisine.*

—*Tony Hendra*

Lizzie Borden took an axe
And gave her mother forty whacks;
When she saw what she had done
She gave her father forty-one!

—late nineteenth-century ballad

No, you can't chop your poppa up in Massachusetts.

—Michael Brown

XIII

THIS IS NO HUMBUG

Memorable Lines from Famous Bay Staters

I hate quotations. Tell me what you know.

—*Ralph Waldo Emerson*

We have learned the answers, all the answers:
It is the question that we do not know.

—*Archibald MacLeish*

Let me keep my mind on what matters, which is my job, which is
mostly standing still and learning to be astonished.

—*Mary Oliver*

To live is so startling it leaves little time for anything else.

—*Emily Dickinson*

Life itself is the proper binge.

—*Julia Child*

In the life of each of us, or so it seems to me, there should be a season for silliness, a springtime for some sloth, nocturnes when exquisite young girls are the cynosures of stag lines.

—*George Frazier*

Life is good.

—*Boston T-shirt*

It is a great art to saunter.

—*Henry David Thoreau*

Fun is good.

—*Theodor Geisel (Dr. Seuss)*

All life is an experiment.

—*Oliver Wendell Holmes, Jr.*

If you take the game of life seriously, if you take your nervous system seriously, if you take your sense organs seriously, if you take the energy process seriously, you must turn on, tune in, and drop out.

—*Timothy Leary*

There is no cure for birth and death save to enjoy the interval.

—*George Santayana*

I'll probably go straight to hell. It might be a nice place, really. So many of my friends are already there.

—Arthur Fiedler

Sin makes its own hell, and goodness is its own heaven.

—Mary Baker Eddy

Life comes before literature, as the material always comes before the work. The hills are full of marble before the world blooms with statues.

—Phillips Brooks

Never write when you can speak. Never speak when you can nod. Never nod when you can wink.

—James Michael Curley

I can never read all the books I want, I can never be all the people I want and live all the lives I want.

—*Sylvia Plath*

There is no Frigate like a Book
To take us Lands away

—*Emily Dickinson*

[The Cat in the Hat] is subversive as hell. I've always had a mistrust of adults.

—*Theodor Geisel (Dr. Seuss)*

A classic is a book that doesn't have to be written again.
—W. E. B. DuBois

I was gravely warned by some of my female acquaintances that no woman could expect to be regarded as a lady after she had written a book.
—Lydia Maria Child, author of The Frugal Housewife

Books are the quietest and most constant of friends; they are the most accessible and wisest of counselors, and the most patient of teachers.
—Charles W. Eliot

It takes a great deal of history to produce a little literature.

—*Henry James*

Don't spoil a good story by telling the truth.

—*Isabella Stewart Gardner*

As scarce as truth is, the supply has always been in excess of the demand.

—*Josh Billings*

Not what you think, not what I think, but what is the truth?

—*Mary Lyon*

Truth is so rare that it is delightful to tell it.

—Emily Dickinson

There is in this world no such force as the force of a person determined to rise. The human soul cannot be permanently chained.

—W. E. B. DuBois

Don't trivialize optimism and hope. It built this country. . . . Don't glorify the naysayers when the yeasayers have been at the center of progress since the beginning of recorded time.

—Governor Deval Patrick

And so, my fellow Americans: ask not what your country can do for you—ask what you can do for your country.

—*President John F. Kennedy*

In sum, most Americans are sensible, good-hearted, and prudent. The issue, then, is whether there is a political party that can welcome them home.

—*Senator Paul Tsongas*

I long to hear that you have declared an independency. And, by the way, in the new code of laws which I suppose it will be necessary for you to make, I desire you would remember the ladies and be more generous and favorable to them than your ancestors. Do not put such unlimited power into the hands of the husbands. Remember, all men would be tyrants if they could.

—*Abigail Adams*

My country has in its wisdom contrived for me the most insignificant office that ever the invention of man contrived or his imagination conceived.

—Vice President John Adams

No man who ever held the office of President would congratulate a friend on obtaining it. He will make one man ungrateful, and a hundred men his enemies, for every office he can bestow.

— President John Adams

Mothers all want their sons to grow up to become president, but they don't want them to become politicians in the process.

—John F. Kennedy

Politics is not the art of the possible. It consists in choosing between the disastrous and the unpalatable.

—John Kenneth Galbraith

The conscious and intelligent manipulation of the organized habits and opinions of the masses is an important element in democratic society.

—Edward Bernays

A democracy is, amongst civilized nations, accounted the meanest and worst of all forms of government.

—John Winthrop

Frankly, I don't mind not being president. I just mind that somebody else is.

—Edward M. Kennedy

Politics is an astonishing profession. It has enabled me to go from being an obscure member of the junior varsity at Harvard to being an honorary member of the Football Hall of Fame.

—John F. Kennedy

You'd be amazed at the number of people who want to introduce themselves to you in the men's room. It's the most bizarre part of this entire thing.

—Presidential candidate John Kerry

But if politics demands hard work and inflicts pain, it also offers an occasional touch of poetry.

—*William M. Bulger*

I think there is too much bloviating around from politicians.

—*Representative Barney Frank*

Whenever you're sitting across from some important person, always picture him sitting there in a suit of long red underwear. That's the way I always operated in business.

—*Joseph P. Kennedy*

Practical politics consists in ignoring facts.

—Henry Adams

I was the seventh of nine children. When you come from that far down you have to struggle to survive.

—Robert F. Kennedy

To me, producing a great son who is an inspiration to many is more exciting that writing a great book or producing a great painting.

—Rose Fitzgerald Kennedy

One of the best things in the world that you can do, is something that your parents think is completely stupid and asinine. Then be really successful at it and have them be proud of you.

—*Jim Koch*

Only those who dare to fail greatly can ever achieve greatly.

—*Robert F. Kennedy*

Not failure, but low aim, is crime.

—*James Russell Lowell*

If you don't fall down, you aren't trying hard enough.

—*Tenley Albright*

Remember, caution can be as much of a problem as freewheelingness.
—*Doris Kearns Goodwin*

An essential aspect of creativity is not being afraid to fail.
—*Edwin Land*

It's just a simple matter of mathematics!
—*Nathaniel Bowditch, on naval navigation*

There are plenty of new ideas just waiting to be recognized.
—*Harold Edgerton*

My conviction is that all humans have the potential to be creative, but only repeated confrontation with the demand to be so exercises and develops the latent capacity.

—*Robert W. Mann*

Gentlemen, this is no humbug.
    —*Dr. John Warren, on the first use of ether as an anesthetic*

Any problem can be solved using the materials in the room.

—*Edwin Land*

I can't tell you if genius is hereditary, because heaven has granted me no offspring.

—*James Abbott McNeill Whistler*

Common sense is instinct, and enough of it is genius.

—*Josh Billings*

Mr. Watson, come here. I want to see you.

—*Alexander Graham Bell*

If you're having problems with technology, you probably figure it's your own fault. But here's the good (and bad) news: It's not. I'm a professor at MIT, but I'm always struggling with gadgets and gizmos.

—*John Maeda*

How you find the valuable kernel of information in a pile of papers on your desk, that's a life skill in the modern world.

—*Pauline Maier*

All progress is experimental.

—*John Chapman*

Wearing traditional witch's robes all the time, I found it difficult to work at IBM.

> —*Laurie Cabot,*
> *Wiccan practitioner and "official witch" of Salem*

It seems that we now use more time and energy on the technology that was supposed to save us time and energy. And every day we get more tools to do things that we don't really want to do but feel dumb for not learning to do. Anybody want to program that?

> —*Ellen Goodman*

If a sales clerk can't explain how to use a gadget in a single breath, it's probably too complicated.

> —*John Maeda*

Television, despite its enormous presence, turns out to have added pitifully few lines to the communal memory.

—*Justin Kaplan*

If Aristotle were alive today he'd have a talk show.

—*Timothy Leary*

There is no reason for any individual to have a computer in his home.

—*Ken Olsen*

The Internet has made joke telling obsolete.
                          —*Moshe Waldoks, co-author of*
              The Big Book of Jewish Humor

There is no other article for individual use so universally known or widely distributed. In my travels I have found [the safety razor] in the most northern town in Norway and in the heart of the Sahara Desert.
                                          —*King Gillette*

Progress in civilization has been accompanied by progress in cookery.
                                       —*Fannie Farmer*

No matter what happens in the kitchen, never apologize.

—*Julia Child*

People form their day-to-day opinions of life through their kitchen window.

—*Representative Joe Moakley*

Life, within doors, has few pleasanter aspects than a neatly arranged and well-provisioned breakfast table.

—*Nathaniel Hawthorne*

Be Mine	Sweet Talk	True Love	I'm Super
Be Good	Fax Me	Ura Star	For You
Be True	Call Me	#1 Fan	
Kiss Me	E-Mail Me	Love Life	

—Conversation Hearts produced by the Massachusetts-based New England Confectionery Company (NECCO) since the early twentieth century

Why don't you speak for yourself, John Alden?
—Priscilla Mullens, responding to Alden's asking for her hand in marriage on behalf of Miles Standish

Marriage, like death, is a debt we owe to nature.
—Julia Ward Howe

We should distrust any enterprise that requires new clothes.
—Henry David Thoreau

Housekeeping ain't no joke!
—Louisa May Alcott

Men their rights and nothing more; women their rights and
nothing less.
—Susan B. Anthony

Women who seek to be equal with men lack ambition.
—Timothy Leary

Normal is getting dressed in clothes that you buy for work and driving through traffic in a car that you are still paying for—in order to get to the job you need to pay for the clothes and the car, and the house you leave vacant all day so you can afford to live in it.

—Ellen Goodman

There must be quite a few things a hot bath won't cure, but I don't know many of them.

—Sylvia Plath

Life is intrinsically, well, boring and dangerous at the same time. At any given moment the floor may open up. Of course, it almost never does; that's what makes it so boring.

—Edward Gorey

If we see light at the end of the tunnel it is the light of an
oncoming train.

—Robert Lowell

We all agree that pessimism is a mark of superior intellect.

—John Kenneth Galbraith

If we had no winter, the spring would not be so pleasant; if we had
not sometimes taste of adversity, prosperity would not be so welcome.

—Anne Bradstreet

There's something really great and romantic about being poor and
sleeping on couches.

—Ben Affleck

There is no secret in fortune making. All you have to do is buy cheap and sell dear, act with thrift and shrewdness and be persistent.

—Hetty Robinson Green

It ain't often that a man's reputation outlasts his money.

—Josh Billings

I now know all the people worth knowing in America, and I find no intellect comparable to my own.

—Margaret Fuller

Egotism: the art of seeing in yourself what others cannot see.

—George V. Higgins

I am confirmed in my division of human energies. Ambitious people climb, but faithful people build.

—*Julia Ward Howe*

A modern, harmonic and lively architecture is the visible sign of an authentic democracy.

—*Walter Gropius*

One is very thankful these days for a concert piece that has a finale one can whistle while leaving the hall.

—*Leonard Bernstein*

Dance is the only art of which we ourselves are the stuff of which it is made.

—*Ted Shawn*

I suppose the picture-habit (which I seem to have) is as bad as the morphine or whiskey one.

—Isabella Stewart Gardner

If merely "feeling good" could decide, drunkenness would be the supremely valid human experience.

—William James

The best way to convince a fool that he is wrong is to let him have his own way.

—Josh Billings

When all is moral chaos, this is the time for you to be a mensch.

—Aaron Feuerstein

You must conduct your lives in such a way that when you come out on the stage to lead your orchestra you can truthfully say to yourself: "Yes, I have the right to appear before these lovers of good music. They can watch me without shame. I have the right because my life and my work are clean."

—Serge Koussevitzky

Study as if you were going to live forever; live as if you were going to die tomorrow.

—Maria Mitchell

I must study politics and war that my sons may have liberty to study mathematics and philosophy. My sons ought to study mathematics and philosophy, geography, natural history, naval architecture, navigation, commerce, and agriculture, in order to give their children a right to study painting, poetry, music, architecture, statuary, tapestry, and porcelain.

—John Adams

I'm someone whose experiences, laid out on paper and in song, somehow supplied people with a language that was helpful to them, and it has put me in the strange position of being the center of attention and still feeling like I lack a center.

—*James Taylor*

What begins in delight ends in wisdom.

—*Robert Frost*

Education, then, beyond all other devices of human origin, is a great equalizer of the conditions of men. . . . It gives each man the independence and the means by which he can resist the selfishness of other men.

—*Horace Mann*

Baseball gives every American boy a chance to excel. Not just to be as good as someone else, but to be better. This is the nature of man and the name of the game.

—*Ted Williams*

I live in a democracy and I believe in democracy, but in sports there can be no democracy, because there simply isn't time for one. The one word I never wanted to hear was why.

—*Red Auerbach*

Without the Hail Mary, I think I would have been easily forgotten. Fame is fleeting, especially for college athletes. I'd probably be just another guy who won the Heisman Trophy.

—*Doug Flutie*

The surest test of discipline is its absence.

—*Clara Barton*

I always believed I could be a starting quarterback in the NFL because I knew I was willing to do whatever was required to get there.

—*Tom Brady*

Running is a way of life for me, just like brushing my teeth. If I don't run for a few days, I feel as if something's been stolen.

—*John A. Kelley*

As a player, I believed in intimidation. I didn't want to just win games, I wanted to rob the other team of any sense of belief they had in their ability. I didn't want players thinking they could come back against us when they were down.

—*Bill Russell*

When going into the ring I have always had it in mind that I would be the conqueror. That has always been my disposition.

—*John L. Sullivan, the Boston Strong Boy*

Part of being a champ is acting like a champ. You have to learn how to win and not run away when you lose.

—*Nancy Kerrigan*

As a pro, winning the championship is the most enjoyable time you're going to have. You want to milk it because you know it's only going to last until the next season gets under way.

—*Larry Bird*

It is harder to stay a champion than it was to get there in the first place.

—*Bill Russell*

I'm a lousy loser. I don't hold with these Pollyanna theories about
the game being the thing.

—*Bob Cousy*

There's no substitute for winning. None. Never forget that.

—*Red Auerbach*

Do you realize that even as we sit here, we are hurtling through
space at a tremendous rate of speed? Think about it. Our world
is just a hanging curveball.

—*Bill Lee*

Do not look at stars as bright spots only. Try to take in the vastness
of the universe.

—*Maria Mitchell*

I imagined how wonderful it would be to make [a] device which had even the possibility of ascending to Mars.

—*Robert H. Goddard*

One world at a time.

—*Henry David Thoreau's last words*

When you have seen one ant, one bird, one tree, you have not seen them all.

—*Edward O. Wilson*

Let's live to be 100 or die trying!

—*Jeff Taylor*

Selected Bibliography

Aerosmith, with Davis, Stephen. *Walk This Way.* New York:
    Avon Books, 1997.

Amory, Cleveland. *The Proper Bostonians.* New York: Dutton, 1947.

Auerbach, Red, with Feinstein, John. *Let Me Tell You A Story.* Boston:
    Little, Brown and Company, 2004.

Benoit, Joan. *Running Tide.* New York: Alfred A. Knopf, 1987.

Berger, Josef. *Cape Cod Pilot.* Boston: Northeastern University Press, 1985.

Beston, Henry. *The Outermost House.* New York: Viking Press,
    1928, 1949, 1956.

Bird, Larry, with Ryan, Bob. *Drive: The Story of My Life.* New York:
    Doubleday, 1989.

Brown, Dona. *Inventing New England.* Washington and London: Smithsonian
    Institution Press, 1995.

Bulger, William M. *While the Music Lasts: My Life in Politics.* Boston: Houghton Mifflin Company, 1996.

Conroy, Frank. *Time & Tide.* New York: Crown Publishers, 2004.

Conway, Jill Ker. *A Woman's Education.* New York: Alfred A. Knopf, 2001.

Cunningham, Michael. *Land's End.* New York: Crown Publishers, 2002.

Dickson, Harry Ellis. *Arthur Fiedler and the Boston Pops.* Boston: Houghton Mifflin Company, 1981.

Faris, John T. *Seeing the Eastern States.* Philadelphia: J.B. Lippincott Company, 1922.

Federal Writers' Project. *The Berkshire Hills.* New York: Duell, Sloan and Pearce, 1939.

Federal Writers' Project. *Massachusetts.* Boston: Houghton Mifflin Company, 1937.

Finch, Robert. *Common Ground: A Naturalist's Cape Cod.* Boston: David Godine, 1981.

Fischer, David Hackett. *Paul Revere's Ride.* New York, Oxford: Oxford University Press: 1994.

Fitch, Noel Riley. *Appetite for Life: The Biography of Julia Child.* New York: Doubleday, 1997.

Fountain, Charles. *Another Man's Poison: The Life and Writing of Columnist George Frazier.* Chester, Connecticut: Globe Pequot Press, 1984.

Goodman, Ellen. *Value Judgments.* New York: Farrar Straus Giroux, 1993.

Green, David. *101 Reasons to Love the Red Sox.* New York: Stewart, Tabori & Chang, 2005.

Hawthorne, Hildegarde. *Old Seaport Towns of New England.* New York: Dodd, Mead & Company, 1916.

Higdon, Hal. *Boston: A Century of Running.* Pennsylvania: Rodale Press, 1995.

DeWolfe Howe, M.A. *Boston: The Place and the People.* London: The Macmillan Company, 1912.

Kenneally, Christopher. *Massachusetts 101: The 101 Events That Made Massachusetts.* Beverly, Massachusetts: Commonwealth Editions, 2005.

Kidder, Tracy. *Home Town.* New York: Random House, 1999.

Kurlanksy, Mark. *Cod: A Biography of the Fish That Changed the World.* New York: Walker and Company, 1997.

Larcom, Lucy. *A New England Girlhood.* Copyright 1889. Reprinted Williamstown, Massachusetts: Corner House Publishers, 1985.

Leno, Jay. *Leading With My Chin.* New York: HarperCollins Publishers, 1996.

Maher, Paul, Jr., ed. *Empty Phantoms: Interviews and Encounters with Jack Kerouac.* New York: Thunder's Mouth Press, 2005.

MacDonald, Michael Patrick. *All Souls.* Boston: Beacon Press, 1999.

Mariani, John F. *Dictionary of American Food and Drink.* New York: Ticknor & Fields, 1983.

McCord, David. *About Boston.* Boston: Little, Brown and Company, 1948.

O'Connell, Shaun. *Imagining Boston: A Literary Landscape.* Boston: Beacon Press, 1990.

O'Connor, Thomas H. *Bibles, Brahmins, and Bosses: A Short History of Boston.* Boston: Trustees of the Boston Public Library, 1991.

Philbrick, Nathaniel. *In the Heart of the Sea: The Tragedy of the Whaleship* Essex. New York: Penguin Books, 2000.

Price, Christopher. *Baseball by the Beach.* Yarmouth Port, Massachusetts: On Cape Publications, 1998.

Root, Waverley and de Rochemont, Richard. *Eating in America.* New York: The Ecco Press, 1976.

Russell, Bill with Faulkner, David. *Russell Rules.* New York: Dutton, 2001.

Shand-Tucci, Douglass. *The Art of Scandal: The Life and Times of Isabella Stewart Gardner.* New York: HarperCollins Publishers, 1997.

Stavely, Keith and Fitzgerald, Kathleen. *America's Founding Food.* Chapel Hill & London: University of North Carolina Press, 2004.